My Life with
TOURETTE'S
SYNDROME

Just a "Tic" Away from Divine Intervention

FAITH STODDARD

ISBN 978-1-0980-8996-2 (paperback)
ISBN 978-1-0980-8997-9 (digital)

Christian Faith Publishing
832 Park Avenue
Meadville, PA 16335
www.christianfaithpublishing.com

Scripture taken from the New King James Version. Copyright © 1982 by Thomas Nelson, Inc., Used by permission. All rights reserved.

Printed in the United States of America

DEDICATION

To my mother Josephine Chirillo, you have been, and continue to be a large portion of strength and encouragement to me. Your radiant love for God and your unstoppable prayers have played a major role in my life circumstances. Without them, I could not have written this book. Your strong faith in God and Savior, Jesus Christ, permeates to all who come in contact with you.

I thank you for the excellent mother you are. Your love never wavers. You are a reflection of Jesus Himself, and it is He I see when I look at you.

CONTENTS

—⁓⁕⁜⁕⁓—

INTRODUCTION

When I decided to write this book, I knew it was going to be one of the hardest things I would ever do, if not the hardest. I knew I had to go out of my comfort zone. I had to have self-discipline. I had to delve into my past and organize my thoughts with detail. I didn't feel that I had the cognitive ability to do all that was required to write a book, but because I felt strongly that the experiences I've had should be shared, I could not dismiss this idea.

This book is solely about my life and the trials I withstood as a child, then as a wife and mother, and now a grandmother and how I have coped and still cope with my neurological disorder today. I believe that what I have experienced in my life and how I have dealt with it are unique.

There are some instances that took place in my life even before adulthood that define who I am today and, to a degree, my characteristics as well. This is not necessarily a good thing, just circumstantial, since these events were out of my control. However, one was of my choosing, and I believe it is the sole reason why I am still here today to write about it.

I lived a good part of my life battling tormenting, irrational fears that haunted me at times with no end. I lived through anxiety and debilitating depression with almost no relief. I coped with bullies at school who made fun of me daily. I did have some good friends, however, and I managed to graduate and go to work like everybody else. But I knew that I was not like everybody else.

I was married at age nineteen. How could a man want to get involved with a person like me even when warned that he didn't truly know who I was and how much I would rely on him more as a father than a husband? Why did things get worse even after I become a Christian? Did God desert me? That's not what my mother taught me, but that's the way it felt to me at the time.

Reading this book could possibly change the way you look at your life and others. Maybe it will nudge you to be more compassionate or more appreciative of life. Maybe you will no longer be so quick to judge people from what you see on the outside. You may know someone who is suffering with some of the issues discussed in this book, or you may be that someone. If so, I hope you will take comfort in knowing that someone else has gone through them and has been stable enough to write about it.

Because I suffered in silence with things that tore at the very core of my being, I could not live my life in any kind of normal fashion. As a mother, I sometimes couldn't take care of my kids, or even myself for that matter, even though this was my heart's desire. I felt worthless and useless. Often I couldn't sleep, but I didn't want to get out of bed. You may be asking yourself, "Why couldn't she just straighten out and be like everyone else?" I asked myself the same question. If only I could have explained to someone what was going on in my head, but I felt nobody would understand. This is depression the way I know it, yet this disorder was not depression itself.

The symptoms for this debilitating disorder began to manifest when I was only four years old. This disorder has a name now—Tourette's syndrome—but it didn't when I was a child. It started one day out of the blue when I began to blink my eyes real hard but couldn't blink them hard enough to satisfy myself. I was making grunting sounds and repeating what people said and twitching my head. I would grunt so hard that my throat was often irritated. Of course, people began to notice and ask me why I was doing this stuff, and all I could say was "I don't know." and I surely didn't.

On the way to school, as I walked, I would get the urge to kick one of my legs with my foot, and then I would have to kick the other leg with the other foot, or I would not feel right. I would feel unbalanced, and it would drive me crazy unless I "completed" the tic only to get the urge again and do the same thing over and over.

I surely didn't know it then, but this disorder and all of its "baggage" would mark my life in a big way. You might be asking yourself, "What good can come of someone who is so messed up, and what good can she be for anybody? How could she get through all those days as a child with kids making fun of her and continuously staring at her, waiting for her next jerky movement? How did her husband tolerate her, and wasn't he embarrassed to be with her in public? Did her kids bring home any friends, or were they too embarrassed? Did she ever suffer rejection from anybody? How did she cope with all the depression, fear, and anxiety?" I've addressed all of these questions in the chapters that follow.

I have had Tourette's syndrome since 1956 but wasn't diagnosed until 1979, and so much has happened to me since then. But so much has also happened for me because of God's providence and promises. You'll read about all of the "to me" and "for me" happenings in this book, and I hope my experiences will encourage you in your most troubled circumstance and help you understand someone with Tourette's that you know or are caring for.

This book reflects my life with Tourette syndrome, OCD, severe anxiety, and depression, along with type 1 diabetes, which was diagnosed when I was thirteen. Truthfully, I never thought I would live this long with all these ailments lying in my path, waiting to destroy me, either through sickness or by literally scaring myself to death. It didn't happen, and there is a reason. God is bigger than any of them put together. I had to learn this as I lived day by day. I am still learning it.

CHAPTER 1

So What Is Tourette's Syndrome?

Tourette's syndrome is a neuropsychiatric syndrome with onset in childhood that is characterized by chronic multiple tics. The cause of Tourette's syndrome is unknown, but the pathophysiology most likely involves basal ganglia and frontal cortical circuits. A useful scheme of basal ganglia dysfunction should be able to account for the features that make Tourette's syndrome unique, in addition to the features that Tourette's syndrome shares with other disorders. Recent advances in knowledge of basal ganglia functional anatomy and physiology make it possible to hypothesize how specific neural mechanisms relate to specific clinical manifestations of Tourette's syndrome. A model of selection and suppression of competing behaviors by the basal ganglia is presented. The functional anatomy of basal ganglia circuits and new information on dopamine modulation of those circuits provide the basis for hypotheses of basal ganglia dysfunction in Tourette's syndrome.

French neuropsychiatrist Georges de la Tourette was an expert on epilepsy, hysteria, and hypnotism but made his most lasting contribution to medicine with an 1884 paper describing nine patients afflicted with involuntary motor and vocal tics, sometimes accompanied by bursts of "notorious cursing." He determined that the disorder usually began in childhood and that more males than females were affected, and in later studies, he found that the ailment is hereditary and not a progressive degenerative disorder, that episodes of uncontrollable spasms usually start in the face or upper extremities, and that the symptoms come and go without warning but that stress or sleep deprivation can make these attacks worse and more frequent. The disease Tourette described is now named for him, Tourette's syndrome.

The onset is usually before the age of eighteen. I was about four or five years old when my symptoms began. They were a display of blinking my eyes, shaking my head, and clearing my throat. I would also bend my body back and forth to get a relieved feeling. I also repeated what other people said (echolalia). Other people in my family noticed my symptoms but tolerated them early in the disorder, simply calling me a "nervous child." That term stuck with me for a good part of my life until I was finally diagnosed. The occurrence of the tics may come many times a day (usually in bouts) and can increase with added stress, anxiety, and fatigue. This means that the tics wax and wane in severity depending on the person's environment.

Sometimes the symptoms can disappear for weeks or months at a time. I don't recall mine ever disappearing for that length of time once they started, but each case is different and unique in the way it takes form. I had the urge to "even things up." For instance, if I blinked just one eye, I had to blink the other eye. This relieved the stress of the "imbalance" I felt until I completed the tic with both eyes. I also developed what is called a "compulsion" to once again even up things by kicking one leg as I walked to school and then feeling the unevenness and having to kick the other leg, once again, to even up the feeling and other ritualistic behaviors that can come in many different forms and done repeatedly, such as touching something with one hand and having to touch it with the other hand. It's that "balance" thing again. I have met people with Tourette's syndrome who had the urge to cross the street and touch complete strangers. This can get quite complicated when it comes to invading someone else's private space.

A person with Tourette's syndrome can also have obsessions. These can be unwanted and/or repetitive thoughts that stay in a person's head. These thoughts are usually bothersome and can cause anxiety and even depression. This symptom was just as much (or more than) an issue with me than the tics themselves. Puberty brought on severe tics, obsessions, and compulsions which made my teenage years very miserable.

Two quite controversial symptoms sometimes displayed in 30 percent of Tourette's patients are coprolalia and copropraxia. Coprolalia is a display of verbal utterances that are obscene and socially inappropriate; copropraxia is a motor tic that involves obscene gestures which are entirely unintentional. I have not had much of an issue with either of these symptoms, but I have discussed my struggle with echolalia in chapter 18. I was able to muffle repeating the sound of a person coughing. Even now, I still get the urge to cough if I hear someone else cough, so I muffle it under my breath. One of my other tics was a forceful broken-up hum which I no longer have.

The tics I have at the present time and have had for most of my life are the head ticking and facial grimaces along with blinking my eyes. I am aware that others with Tourette's syndrome have more than just a few tics, and I consider myself fortunate to have come this far in life with this disorder and all of its complexities.

ADD or ADHD can precede children with Tourette's syndrome with signs of hyperactivity showing up before TS symptoms appear. This can make it difficult to conclude a diagnosis, but time usually will tell whether a child really has Tourette's syndrome simply by its unique display of symptoms which cannot be explained away. In my situation, neither I nor anyone else ever realized that the facial and body tics could have been related to my other odd behavior, such as obsessive compulsive thinking, depression, and irrational fears, all of which I displayed along with the head ticking and all other tics. You see, what was going on inside my head was even worse than what I was doing with my head. Even as I got older and the depression, fears, and OCD were fiercely taking a toll on me, I never connected them with the visible tics.

Tourette's syndrome is an overly complex disorder and can be quite devastating to a family before the diagnosis is made, but that can take a long time. After the diagnosis, a treatment plan for medication may be implemented, and school officials should be notified and educated on Tourette's syndrome so the child can have a support system while at school and at home. Today it is that way, and children are less devastated because we have knowledge and understanding through education that was not available in my time.

Homeschooling is an option that could provide the perfect environment for a child with Tourette's syndrome because he or she would not have interference from kids or even teachers who may lack the ability (out of ignorance of the disorder) to tolerate a child with TS. This is one disorder that attracts people in general, but bullies could have a field day with this because of all the different symptoms exhibited in a child with Tourette's syndrome.

If a child with Tourette's syndrome has a positive home life where he or she is valued and has a strong support system, then public school could be a positive choice. Education about Tourette's syndrome is more available today, and it is getting better and better. But there is still more work to be done about educating the public.

A child who has been diagnosed with Tourette's syndrome and goes to public school can educate his peers, teachers, and administrators because he or she has the knowledge of what and why they are ticking. For example, a child can get permission to hold an assembly and explain to the whole school at once about Tourette's syndrome. TV programs like Oprah and other talk shows have brought this disorder into the limelight. Movies have been made about Tourette's syndrome, and all this exposure has been beneficial to parents and their children with Tourette's syndrome. But a lot more needs to be done.

Someone finally did approach me later in life with vital information to share with me about my tics, and it turned out that her suspicions were correct. The information she gave me led to my diagnosis, and for the first time, I was able to have a name for my condition which liberated me to be able to talk about my disorder without embarrassment and educate people with knowledge and information which I was not able to do before. This diagnosis marked the end of telling people "I don't know" when asked about the tics.

This was a very liberating experience because it gave me ammunition up against the sometimes cruel world I was living in.

CHAPTER 2

Life in the Projects: Where It All Started

I was born in Stamford, Connecticut in 1952. My mother, Josephine, and father, Pasquale (known to friends and family as Joyce and Pat), are both Italian. I was the baby of the family, having two older siblings and, later in life, pleasantly surprised to have two other siblings on my father's side, plus one more on my mother's side.

I didn't know it then, but we were poor. So we had to move to  project housing when I was just three years old. There were four large, red-brick buildings that were eight stories high, and each building housed eighty-eight families. They were brand spanking new and quite a step up from our former rented house from what I was told. I remember my father walking us through our unit, trying to convince my mother of how much better off we were as he felt the warm doorknobs from the baseboard heat. The walls were cinder block with a coat or two of greenish-grayish paint throughout the unit.

There was one small bedroom downstairs and two upstairs. One would be my brother's room, which had a metal-framed window that directly faced one of the other project buildings. Just across the little hall was the other bedroom, which had a picturesque view of I-95 (known as the thruway). That was the girls' bedroom. When I got older, I got the bedroom downstairs. I didn't like that because it was scary to wake up alone in the middle of the night. When I did, I would run upstairs as fast as I could and slide in between my mother and sister. Then I would feel safe again.

My mother and father were separated, for lack of a better word. That's the way it always was. I didn't know at the time that there was any different way one's parents lived. I did eventually figure out that we were the unusual ones, not the other way around. I did love my father very much, and when he would come home, I can remember jumping up to hug him as if he was a soldier returning from war. When he would leave the house, I would stare out the living room window until I could see him no longer.

I missed him immensely and would not go anywhere when he came home so I could see him as much as possible. He had a temper, and his face would turn bright red when he got upset. So my mother knew to get us out of his way, and she would take us upstairs where we wouldn't have to see or hear him yell. Not having his complete love and attention, which I so desperately needed as a little girl, did affect me when I started to get interested in boys. I had no idea then, but now I know and understand how vital a good father-daughter relationship is to a growing child.

A mother simply cannot make up for the absence of a father, although sometimes it cannot be helped that a dad isn't in the picture. If a child knows that they are loved, accepted, and cherished, and for some reason cannot have contact with their dad, that is different. I am speaking here of situations like death, military separation, or sickness.

A father is usually the first man a daughter loves, and the role model he plays in her life is going to make a difference (in most cases) as to the choices she will make as she becomes a young lady. It's an awesome responsibility and one that my own father failed to meet.

My mother is, to me, one of the most wonderful people on earth. She is so loving, kindhearted, caring, and self-sacrificing. She basically raised us in a low-income neighborhood without any emotional or financial support from my father. She had her work cut out for her, and she met every demand. She fed us homecooked meals, ironed our clothes, made sure we got to school, and took us to church. She also took on cleaning jobs that were located in rich neighborhoods like Old Greenwich, which meant she would have to take a bus to and from her cleaning job and be home before we returned from school. She never complained or spoke badly about my father in any way. Where did her strength come from? I didn't know then, but I know now. Anybody would have cracked under the pressure she was under. And maybe she did sometimes, but not in front of us.

Life in the "village" (as we called it) was good. We had a grassy field in which to play baseball in the summertime. And there was no shortage of kids to play with as the four buildings filled up with tenants. There was a mom-and-pop candy store about a quarter of a mile away where we could buy our penny candy and those nickel candy bars. Through the hot and humid summers, the ice-cream man would come several times a day. At times, three ice cream trucks would show up all at once. I would usually get a chocolate soft-serve cone. It cost ten cents then. And no sooner than it was made and handed to me, it often would fall on the ground from melting at record speed from the heat and humidity. But I would go back, and the nice man would refill my cone without charge.

I loved to catch lightning bugs in a jar and watch them light up. I played marbles in the dirt with my brother and all the neighbor kids. I played hopscotch and hide-and-seek. We played baseball until we could not see in the dark anymore. My brother loved animals and birds. Some summer mornings, we would wake up and catch pigeons by taking a cardboard box, a piece of string, and a stick. We would tie the string to the stick and raise the box up. When a pigeon flew in, we would pull the string. My brother often brought home baby birds that would die if we did not nurse them back to life. We would put them near the gas stove and turn it on so they could have heat. Then he would feed them milk with an eyedropper. This was all fun to watch when I was a kid, but I wonder where those birds ever ended up.

The Multipurpose Stairway

There was no one more excited than I when a thunderstorm was coming. The sky would darken until it looked like nighttime in the middle of the day. To this day, I am still thrilled when there is going to be a thunderstorm, blizzard, or windstorm. At that time, my mother would yell to us, "Run upstairs and close all the windows!" But because the windows had metal frames, I was convinced that if I touched them when lightning was striking, I would get electrocuted; thus, I always hated to be the one to have that dangerous task. Our stairway had side walls (those cinder block ones I mentioned), and once you started to ascend, you couldn't see anything on either side except the landing at the top of the stairs. Because of that, my mother would take us kids and walk halfway up the stairs and then sit down with us until the storm passed. We would hear the thunder crack and prepare ourselves for the big *boom* but never see the lightning, and we were so comforted while sitting on those stairs with her, seeking shelter from the storm. I know now that had she not been there with us in the stairway, we would have been frightened even though we were protected from the lightning. Yes, it was her presence that comforted us. She told us that thunder was God moving furniture around in heaven. And of course, I believed it.

I had a lot of cousins who lived nearby, and sometimes on that same stairway, we would play a game called "hide the button." The game started with two or three of us sitting down on the first step. Then one of us would stand up and hide a button in one of our hands, and sitters would take turns guessing which hand the button was in. Whoever guessed right would move up one step. The first to reach the top of the stairs was the winner. But if one of us was almost to the top of the stairway and guessed wrong down we went to start all over. We played for hours on those stairs.

Christmas was a happy time, for the most part. As Christmas drew near, more and more families in the buildings would string Christmas lights on their windows. My favorite thing to do then was to go in my brother's room when he wasn't around and look outside his window and count how many windows had Christmas lights. It would make me happy when I would see one window after another get Christmas lights. The Christmas tree was always loaded with presents.

Most people in my neighborhood were Catholic. We were not, but I had a Catholic girlfriend. So what do two nine-year-old girls play when it's raining outside? The correct answer is nun school. Marie and I were nuns, and we walked around our classroom (my bedroom) with kerchiefs hanging from the top of our heads and draped over our shoulders. We held them up with a bobby pin, trying to look as much like a nun as we could. The floor in my bedroom happened to be a dark tile, so we used it for our blackboard. When I think of it now, I realize that we actually walked on our blackboard. Our students were there too (in our imaginations, of course.) We split the room in half with a piece of chalk so we could each have our own class. We were the bossiest, meanest nuns that ever lived. We spent most of our time yelling at the "badly behaved children." I remember it all just like it was yesterday.

Unfortunately, what I also remember is the onset of the symptoms which I began to exhibit. I began blinking uncontrollably, grunting, shaking my head, moving my lower body from side to side, shrugging my shoulders, and repeating what other people were saying (out loud or in my head), which is called echolalia. When these symptoms came on, one would replace another for a while, but the head ticking was never replaced with another tic. To this day, I still shake my head.

CHAPTER 3

The Unforgettable Orphan: A Tribute to Lucy Sileo

I was about eight years old and still living in the projects when I met a family that was moving in our building. They were a married couple with a son about three years old. The lady was short in stature, kind of stocky. She may have been pregnant. She had pitch-black hair down to her chin, kind of wavy and page boy style. I felt compelled to go over to talk to her, so I did. She had a French accent. As it turned out, after she got moved in, she and my mother had met over her three-year-old son being found naked in a water hole outside our kitchen window. He

was rescued, and that was the beginning of a unique and lasting friendship between her family and ours.

Lucy is that one person you meet in life and realize there's no one else quite like her. She was the nicest lady I had ever met. Generous, friendly, caring, and funny are four adjectives that described her; and that combination of personality traits made her very popular with the kids in the neighborhood. Whenever those ice-cream trucks rolled into the parking lot, she didn't think twice about giving any child a dime to buy a cone if they didn't have one. She would play games with us that she learned at the orphanage where she had lived. An orphan since infancy, she was left on the steps of the orphanage and never left until she took her first job as a governess. She told stories about her childhood that I'll never forget. I came to love this lady, and we had a special relationship over time. Each day after school was over, I would go home and then dash up the seven flights of stairs where she lived, which happened to be directly over our apartment.

Lucy trusted me like I was her own daughter. She played the mother role when we were together, and I was delighted to be in her company. It wasn't because I didn't love my own mother; I loved her, but Lucy was different. She was the one who became concerned about my ticking and blinking and talked my mother into having me checked. That got me a trip to the hospital for blood tests, a brain-wave, and neck x-rays. I remember the day we found out the results of the tests. The phone rang. My mother picked it up, and her countenance began to change as she was told the delightful news that all the tests were normal. She hung up the phone and told me the results and then took my hand; and suddenly, we were dancing in circles and singing something, overjoyed that all the tests were normal, well, almost. The blood work showed that I was anemic, so I had to start taking multiple vitamins.

If you grew up in the fifties, you should remember Chocks multiple vitamins. Every morning just before walking out the door to go to school, I would chew up a Chocks. These vitamins may have helped my blood count to return to normal, but they didn't help me in school, where I dreaded to be. At school, I was often ridiculed by children and most of my teachers for my "nervous twitch." I remember my first-grade teacher yelling at me because I didn't understand the instructions on a test, therefore, holding up the rest of the class.

I often was so embarrassed that I wished I could just disappear. I was convinced that I was stupid. I think I convinced myself of that with a little help from the children and adults who ridiculed me. Ironically, I never ran out of a classroom or retaliated for any of the verbal abuse. I never even told my mother what was happening to me in school. I would just come home and run up to Lucy's apartment. She never made fun of me, and she was my safety zone away from the world outside.

By now, Lucy had given birth to another son whose name was Jimmy Joseph. I would get to be his big sister. He was like a little brother to me, as was her first son Lucy had a ringer-type washing machine like most people did then. When she wasn't looking, I would look for the baby's rubber pants washing in the machine. Then I would pull them out of the machine and put them through the ringer until they formed a bubble, and I waited impatiently for the loud pop as soon as they finished going through the ringer. I think the expression, "They put me through the ringer," must have come from those machines. Also, on occasion, I would open a little jar of baby food and eat it. I later confessed my "sins" to Lucy, and we had a good laugh about it.

She had another child, a girl named Michelle. Even to this day, she is like the little sister I never had. Soon after that, Lucy and her family moved out of the village into another housing project about two miles away. I missed her tremendously, but I would go to her house on Saturdays and spend the whole day there.

Call it a coincidence—I call it divine intervention—but it wasn't long before my family moved, and we ended up on the very same street, almost directly across from each other. She moved again, and we moved again. And we were only one mile away from each other at that time. Then I got married in 1971 and moved to South Carolina and then to Washington State.

By now, our families had become interwoven tightly together in the day-to-day issues of life's ups and downs. Unfortunately, there were many downs on the agenda of life for the Sileo family. In the meantime, my life away from home was another story, and I hadn't realized the trials and heartaches that Lucy and her family were facing. When we would go home for a visit, she would welcome my husband and children into her most humble home and cook up a delicious leg of lamb with all the trimmings. Other times, it would be meatballs and sausage, and she would always serve it up with a smile. The kids were all grown, but she still loved me. And we would reminisce about the old times.

The years went by, and my few-and-far-between visit home and our phone calls to each other kept us updated on what life was doling out to each of us. Lucy was always deeply concerned for the things that were happening in my life and how I was coping, which you will read about in coming chapters. One day, she said to me in her very prominent French accent, "Fay, you got to write a booke." I heard this repeated to me so many times through the years that I got sick of hearing it. But I never totally gave up the idea.

Sadly, Lucy's second son, Jimmy, became very ill and passed away in 1993. Soon afterward, she moved to Spokane, Washington, to be close to her daughter. She was now on one side of the Cascade Mountains, and I was on the other side, close to Seattle. But geographical distance could never come between two old friends like us, so we still visited each other at least three times a year. Besides, we knew that eternity with God was where we would both end up anyway and that one of us would just follow the other as we have been doing all along on planet earth. Our visits to each other's houses drew our relationship closer together as it was before I moved away from Stamford, and I began to enrich my friendship with Michelle now living in Spokane, whom I have adopted as my little sister in my heart.

Then the unthinkable happened. Lucy's firstborn son passed away, deepening the hole already there from losing her younger son. I thought this would eventually be the end of her as I knew her, vibrant and funny with a strong will to live and love others and life itself. But in due time, she once again became victorious over the sadness and grief and was able to smile and laugh again. If you had asked her then, she would have told you only of how good God had been to her and how He had restored her as only He can. I marvel at the strength this woman possessed as she was also dealing with her own physical ailments, which included diabetes. Her spirit soared beyond all of her past and present trials because she had the true One in her heart. Only He gives abundant joy, and He is Jesus.

In October 2010, Lucy was diagnosed with pancreatic cancer and was given two months to live. For the very short time I was with her in November of that year, my heart broke to see the unpleasant symptoms typical of pancreatic cancer and her suffering in pain. I also saw something else I'll never forget. That was the strength that came to her daughter, Michelle, in ways that expressed to Lucy and all that were observing just how much she was loved by her daughter. The love between the two of them was so evident and such a testimony of God's grace in time of need.

Expressing love in the deepest form is not glamorous, exciting, and full of warm fuzzy feelings. It is expressed by hours of sleeplessness, tending to all the personal needs and doling out medication to help the pain and suffering. It is watching your loved one go from a vibrant human being to their utmost misery and still be able to smile, hide the tears, and hold their hand and caress them. This describes the daughter that helped her mother finish her race in this life, literally right down to her very last breath. I am so grateful that I was able to observe the love of God in such depth, and may His grace carry you and me as far as we need to go in our life's journeys.

Lucy was the first person who noticed my ticking and convinced my mother to have tests done. She also was the first person who strongly suggested that I write a book. I will be ever grateful for her suggestion. Lucy, I have finally written "dat booke." I know you would be proud of me. I'll see you again soon. Maybe we will live next door to each other, just like old times. I hope you're behaving up there, but I doubt it. So long for now, dear Lucy.

CHAPTER 4

My Closet Fortress

It would still be about one more year before we would move on Fairfield Avenue, and I was still in the sixth grade and living in the projects in Stamford. This would be my last year in elementary school, and what a last year it was. Most of my teachers were pretty tolerable of the tic movements which were mainly twitching my head in one direction while blinking. I know how ugly it looks to distort my face, and sometimes I wondered how people tolerated me at all.

I remember one very disturbing thing happening in third grade. Why it came and why it went away, I don't know to this day, but I had an unrealistic fear that some of the teachers were planning to take me to a nuthouse facility. I really believed this, and every time my teacher stepped out of the class, I thought she was going away to talk and plan with other teachers about my exit from school and into the nuthouse facility. My heart would race, and I would break out in a sweat from the fear. What I don't understand when I think of this now is that she was one of the nicest teachers I had, and she was very tolerant of me. Looking back on it today, I can almost say that it was a form of paranoia. Now, all I am sure of is that it scared the life out of me because I really believed what my mind was telling me. Thankfully, I never had that particular experience again. Ironically, when I got engaged to my husband, this teacher saw the announcement in the local paper and remembered me and sent me a card of congratulations. I guess it wouldn't be very hard to forget a student who shook her head for nine months, but I'm happy to say I was wrong about the nuthouse.

Unlike my third-grade teacher mentioned above, the word *tolerant* would not describe my sixth-grade teacher by a long shot. It would be more like "mad woman." To make it worse, this was probably the time that puberty was beginning to manifest not only in me but the other kids as well; and hormones were dominating our thoughts and actions and playing havoc with the Tourette's in my situation, thus making my tics even more noticeable. By then, the vocal tics and the head jerking had increased, and although she never warned me not to jerk or say things out loud before, one day, she just couldn't take any more of me. From her desk, she yelled in a very loud voice, "Faith, quit shaking your head!" Everybody in the class heard what she said, and a silence overtook the room. I wanted to become invisible again, and this time, she made sure I did. She ordered me to take my desk and chair and go into the closet. So I did, and that's where I stayed for the rest of the day.

Now this closet was where all the students hung their coats. Yes, it smelled in there of armpit negligence. After all, it was sixth grade, and some kids were into puberty but not into deodorant. Going into the closet became a regular thing. It was either the closet, the hallway, or up in front of the class with my desk and chair, which was the worst of the three choices because everybody had a bird's-eye view of me; and that put enormous stress on me, resulting in more severe ticking.

I actually liked it in the closet because I was all alone, and nobody could watch me as I ticked away. I would finally calm down and give myself a break. I can understand how hard it must have been to have a student with such a disruptive problem. Now that I'm grown, I can put myself in her place because I have worked with ADD/ADHD special ed students while employed with the school district in years past, and it wasn't a cakewalk. I know now that sixth grade is a hard grade to teach with students coming into their own, but none of the students took a liking to this particular teacher because she was unpleasant most of the time. It appears she walked around with a chip on her shoulder waiting for someone to knock it off, and I was hired for the job.

One day, she threatened to throw all the girls' pocketbooks out the window if they were brought to school the next day, but she didn't come through on her threat. We even gave her a surprise birthday party which we planned out thoroughly. Someone brought in a record player. Another brought in the 45s. I remember that we had a cake and some food, but now I'm asking myself why. Thinking back, we were probably sucking up to her so she'd be nice to us, or maybe we just wanted an excuse to have some fun. I often brought her Mary Janes, leaving them on her desk as I came into class.

It was no surprise that I would have to go to summer school that year for reading and math. One thing I know for sure was that I was a darn good speller, but that was about all I can claim. It was my cognitive skills that were my weakness. The need to tic or move all the time makes it very hard to concentrate, and that was most of my academic problem. If I caught kids laughing at me or whispering about me, it got my attention, and I couldn't do my work until they stopped.

Sixth grade came and went, and I did survive it, but barely. I went to summer school for six weeks and hated every hot and humid day of it. Today, if a teacher ordered a student to take their desk and chair and go in the clothes closet for the rest of the day, the press would be all over it the next morning, not so, back in the fifties.

This may sound weird, but I am glad that I had that closet to go into because it became my fortress from a cruel and unfriendly environment for just a little while.

CHAPTER 5

I'm So Sweet I Can Just Die

In the introduction of this book, I mentioned things that would define my life. Most of them would not be of my choosing. One of them, of course, is the Tourette's syndrome coming on at about age four and still exhibiting symptoms now at my present age of sixty-nine, which pretty much tells me that I will have this for the rest of my life. The next major event will stay with me for the rest of my life also.

It started happening in the first part of the eighth grade. I was a typical teenager (except for the Tourette's syndrome and all that it came with). Junior high school was very hard for me. It was about this time that my family moved across the street from my dear friend Lucy and her family. I had survived the projects, and now we were renting an old two-story house with a wide porch and white pillars. Although it was an old house with the gray paint chipping off of the porch with white pillars, it was s step up from project living. I could look out of my living room window and see inside of Lucy's house if I looked to the left, and she had her curtains up. Better yet, I didn't have to climb seven flights of stairs to see her. I just had to cross the very narrow street and walk up a few stairs.

By the fall of 1965, I began to notice that I was losing weight and having to take my jeans in. My legs were already skinny. As a matter of fact, I was skinny all over and couldn't afford to lose any weight. I began to get extremely thirsty and very tired. I was very thirsty in school that I couldn't wait to get my half pint of milk so I could chug it down only to find out that I was just as thirsty as I was before the milk. I just could not quench my thirst. I would have to go to the bathroom after every period. One day, I was so thirsty that I chugged down a whole can of Hi-C juice. My mother knew something was wrong, so off I went to the doctor. All he said was that I was anemic and to feed me liver. I could barely tolerate the smell of it being cooked, let alone get it to my mouth to eat it.

Lucy was in the habit of trying to make me healthy, so she would buy chocolate swirl dixie cups for me to eat, thinking that I would start to gain weight again. She nor my mother didn't realize that the ice cream was making me more sick. I came home from school one day and told my mother that I couldn't go anymore because I was too exhausted. I had to stop to catch my breath often, and I was drinking water at every fountain I passed by. All I wanted to do was sleep, and I did.

I eventually got admitted to the hospital. By then, my heartburn was so bad, but nothing took it away. My thirst was endless. But this would end soon. They diagnosed me with type 1 diabetes. I immediately began to receive insulin shots, and to my surprise, I was feeling better in about two days. About the third day, my doctor walked in and simply told me that I had type 1 juvenile diabetes and that I would have to take insulin shots every day for the rest of my life. I took it in stride. I remained in the hospital for about three weeks. I was also in the pediatric ward. I had a black and white TV and remember watching Soupy Sales every afternoon while eating supper.

I had to learn to give myself injections. That wasn't too much of a problem, but my mother had to learn too (on me). When the real test came for her to inject me with saline and a real needle, I was petrified. She did okay, but let's just say that I was the shot giver when I came home.

Looking back on it now, I feel bad because she really went through a lot with being a single parent and having to be my caregiver then and make sure that I took my shots and ate all of my food which she fixed for me. She did a great job, and I didn't complain. Neither did she, ever.

The Night She Walked on Water

It was midwinter when I was in the hospital; and one night, when my mother knew I wasn't going to have visitors because only parents and grandparents could visit, she came. It was below freezing outside, and there was a sheet of ice on the ground. The hospital was about two miles from our house; and yet she walked in the dark, on solid ice, to come and see me She wasn't wearing flat shoes but pumps which she wore all the time. She told me she never took her feet of the ground. She slid there. She also had to walk back. I never forgot that deed she did for me. So you see, she did walk on water. It was just frozen.

I later learned that my blood sugar level was 1,200 when I entered the hospital. I could have died, but God spared me. When I think of how sick I was and bad I felt, I thank my God that He chose to let me live, and that was not the only time He let me live.

One day, soon after coming home from the hospital, I was scheduled to go for a blood sugar test. This was a fasting blood sugar, so I could not eat breakfast until after the blood was drawn. I walked to the hospital, got the test, and walked home. I took my insulin but neglected to eat my breakfast. I also didn't eat any lunch. By now, I should have been feeling low blood sugar but did not. I went through the day. And then right before suppertime, I asked my mother to throw two sugar packets at me, and she did. As I opened it up to put it in my mouth, I passed out. When my mother found me, I just stared at her nonresponsively. I was in insulin shock. I went in an ambulance to the hospital ER where they injected me with some form of sugar in my veins.

I finally did come around, but this could have killed me. I think of this incident as a miracle just as I did when my blood sugar was at 1,200 and not dying or even going into a diabetic coma. This incident taught me a valuable lesson—to take my insulin *and* eat. These incidents are certainly God's miracles, and I am grateful that I learned quick not to be irresponsible with this disease. I also learned that low blood sugar felt terrible, and I would do anything to avoid it.

After almost three weeks, I returned back to school in the eighth grade. I experienced low blood sugar attacks often as I was learning how to adjust my food intake to my insulin. This was not easy. In 1965, testing blood sugar was very primitive, but it's all I had. I had a test tube, an eyedropper, and Clinitest tablets. I would take five drops of urine, ten drops of water and put it in the test tube, then drop the Clinitest tablet in the tube. When it stopped fizzling, I would compare the color it turned against the paper chart to evaluate how much sugar was in my blood. The test was not very accurate. It was like using a thermometer without the mercury.

I owned only one glass needle and had to sterilize it each morning by boiling it in a pan. The needle tips were separate and had to be boiled also. I often wonder how I got through those years, but I didn't complain because I was happy to be alive and feeling normal again. My dear mother (104 years old now) deserved a medal for how she cared for me and did it all without my father around and no car. She didn't have her license and walked everywhere she had to go. She was and still is a gift from God Himself.

CHAPTER 6

Checks and Balances

I had type 1 diabetes for about a year and was in the ninth grade when I began to experience irrational fears, such as the fear of having a brain tumor. I was afraid to tell anyone about my fear, so I kept it locked up inside me until I got to the point where I couldn't keep the fear in any longer and finally told my mother about it. She did the motherly thing by telling me that everybody has fears and that I should not worry because I didn't have a brain tumor. It didn't help at all because I was still totally convinced that I had one.

This was followed by sudden obsessive-compulsive behavior. I began to have the urge to count such things as the stuff on my dresser, like bottles of perfume, deodorant, or bobby pins. It really didn't matter what it was. If it was there on the dresser, I had to count it so I could know how many total items were there. And I had to remember the count inside my head. Also, there had to be the exact number of things on the left side as on the right side. Then I developed another compulsive behavior soon after. I would have to remember the pieces of clothing in my closet, and even stranger than that, I had such an urge to remember the names on each zipper on my dresses. If I forgot what the name said, I would have to get back out of bed and reread it and remember it.

The urge to get out of bed and check things over and over again was so strong that I lost a lot of sleep doing this for the time that it lasted. Also, my school papers had to be in a certain order, and I had to remember the order that they were all in. Or I would have to delve back into my notebook and check again to remember. This often led to checking and double-checking other papers in my notebook, and this went on until I would be very exhausted. It was the same with my schoolbooks. I would have to go back and read over and over what I had already read just to make sure I'd read all the data and hadn't missed anything. That may seem very strange—and it was—but it was either that or burst.

The urge to keep checking information was kind of like ticking. If I didn't do it, I felt like I would go crazy. This craziness took up so much precious time, and I began to feel isolated from everybody, even my own family members. This led to depression and withdrawal. Although I felt so abnormal and threatened by my own compulsive behavior, I could not bring myself to tell anybody.

Because of the Tourette's tics and the diabetes with compulsive behavior, school in the eighth and ninth grades were very hard to cope with. I didn't have any dreams for my future, and I didn't know what it held for me. I was not competitive in anything like sports or music, although I always wanted to be a singer and dancer. I never wanted to join a club or be on a committee because I didn't think I was smart enough. I struggled with comprehension and had low self-esteem. I was afraid of everything and mostly everybody at this time in my life. I took up smoking, and by the time I quit, I smoked three packs a day.

By the time I was age fourteen, I had lived through a lot, but it felt like I was just existing. I thank God for His hand on me through it all. I didn't know then that God Almighty was walking with me everywhere I walked and knew everything I was experiencing, but I know it now. As I was taught as a child, He is a very big God. I memorized the twenty-third psalm when I was only two and a half. That was the doing of my Christian mother whose vocabulary often included the Word of God whether we liked it or not.

CHAPTER 7

Never My Love

If it were not for the fact that I fell in love, high school would have been a more fruitful experience. When I "fell," I fell to the point of almost becoming self-destructive. This rough-and-tumbled relationship went on from the beginning of high school until well into 1970, but I was living a lie in more than one way.

It was the fall of 1967, and only the second day of school when I met this very attractive boy in the guidance councilor's office while standing in line. His name was Danny. After striking up a conversation, we had our first date. I was very attracted to him and liked his blond hair, blue eyes, and nice physique. He was soft-spoken, polite, very reserved, and neatly dressed. Soon we were going steady, and I was wearing his ID bracelet.

After school, he worked at his dad's bicycle shop. He seemed to be self-disciplined, which was how he lived day-to-day. How could I not fall for this guy? He was such a refreshing difference from all the other guys at school, and that made me feel attracted to him even more. I didn't feel at all like I deserved him because I was keeping secrets from him, in particular, my diabetes and the ticking episodes.

I felt so guilty and ashamed, knowing that I was deceiving him and fearing that he would see me twitch my head (which I felt distorted my face to such an ugly, out-of-control maniac) and would wonder who I really was and where I'd come from. Yet this didn't stop me from seeing him. Another fear that engulfed me was that someone who knew of me and of my head tics would tell him that I shook my head all the time and might ask him why I did it. I finally did decide to tell him about the diabetes, but not willingly. While talking to him on the phone one night, I finally told him that I was a diabetic. In my opinion, his reaction was over the top. He immediately went into a very sympathetic tone of voice with a comment something like, "Oh no, you poor thing. That's too bad." I would rather have heard him say, "Oh, you do? Well, there are worse things to have than diabetes."

Then he asked me if I was a Christian. I said yes because I knew he was a Christian, and that's what he wanted to hear. Actually, I was confused as to whether I was a Christian or not because I was not attending church or doing any of the things Christians do; and I was also doing things Christians usually don't do, like wearing short skirts, makeup, smoking cigarettes, and listening to rock and roll music.

Besides that, I was being totally dishonest in not telling him that I shook my head back and forth all the time for no apparent reason. He was so far from being a weirdo, and I wasn't about to let him see me ticking if I could help it. While still on the phone, he asked me if I wouldn't mind going to his church Sunday night and getting prayed for about my diabetes. He believed that I could be healed. Oh, I would have loved to be healed from the diabetes, so I agreed to go even though I didn't think this would help. I was always a pushover and had a tendency to let other people run my life, and this is one of those times.

We went to church that Sunday night, and when the regular service was over, it was time for the prayer service. Did I mention that this was a Pentecostal church? Now I was raised in the Salvation Army church where they don't do any speaking in tongues or laying on of hands, so I was not accustomed to this form of worship. In any event, there I was, up front and center where people gathered all around me. They knew ahead of time what I was being prayed for and that Danny was my boyfriend. They began to pray, and some cried and spoke in tongues. As for me, I just stood there until what seemed like a nightmare was over. I was so uncomfortable because I didn't know how I should react. It wasn't soon enough before they all began to leave, and I could go home.

Of course, I went home with my diabetes, but I know it wasn't because of anybody's lack of faith (except for mine, maybe), but I believe that God had reasons for not healing me that night. I continued to go to church with Danny on Sunday nights but only because I wanted to be with him, not with God. I understand now that God is sovereign and will do what He pleases and what gives Him glory. He will be glorified in my life but not because he healed my diabetes.

Walking on Eggshells

I had always wanted to become a nurse, so when the school offered a nurse aide class, I signed up for it. I ticked a lot in this particular class, perhaps because of pressure to perform. The teacher seemed very unfriendly to me, in particular, and I felt it was because of my severe ticking. I knew she wanted me out of there the day she told me I should quit the class and take another one. After I realized how she felt about me, I felt so belittled and stupid that I knew I had to leave. You think I would've known better and not said anything, but I told Danny what had happened, and he wanted to go talk to the teacher to get to the bottom of it. Then I panicked. I thought, *This is it.* Once he learns the truth of why she wanted me out of there, he'll know about my ticking. Somehow, I convinced him to stay out of it, and he honored my request. A close call, indeed! This is what it was like every day at school. I never knew if someone would tell him about me or make fun of me in the hallways when we were walking together. I had an enormous amount of guilt, keeping all this from him when he didn't deserve it, but I couldn't seem to break up with him or tell him about my problems. How on earth could I have done this to him? Was this love, selfishness, or both?

I was very possessive of Danny, and this was what began to make him distance himself from me. The relationship went on like this for quite some time, and I only cared about the next time I could see him besides just in school. There were times when weeks and months went by before we were together on a date, and it was tearing me apart. My life felt empty without him, but it should not have been. If he called on the phone suddenly and wanted to see me, the answer was always yes!

I had another close call of him finding out about my tics. His sister-in-law saw me at a parade in my hometown, but I didn't see her. I was obviously ticking a lot that day. She saw the display and reported to Danny that I was shaking my head back and forth for some reason. I must have given her some show because I well remember that day at the parade. Loud places where there are a lot of people, kids yelling, music, and confusion always make me tic more than usual.

When we were there at Danny's brother's house to babysit for their kids, he came right out and said to me, "My sister-in-law saw you at the parade yesterday, and she said you were shaking your head. Why were you doing that?" I immediately panicked, and the next thing I knew, I was making up a big lie. I said to him, "Oh, that was when my blood sugar got low, and I began to shake. And so I ate an orange, and it went away." I actually used my diabetes to cover up for the Tourette's syndrome. I guessed he bought it because he didn't say anything else, but I was not proud of myself for lying to him. In fact, I felt awful inside.

As time went by and the seasons changed, everything changed for me when Danny announced that he was going to live in Florida and would be leaving soon. My heart did a flop and felt as though it had dropped down to my stomach. Right then and there, my world began to fall apart. But there was a consolation prize. He said he would return after the school year was over, but I was not consoled. I had fallen in love with this boy, his mannerisms, his smile, his laugh, his voice—his beautiful singing voice—his character, even his chipped tooth. How could I just tuck it away like an old pair of shoes?

When we kissed goodbye, the tears flooded downstream like Snoqualmie Falls in the spring. The love I felt for him was more than I could bear, and the thought of having to leave him and start living my life without him from that moment on was almost impossible for me to grasp. His best friend, Jake, was there with me, and he drove me home. Life did go on, but just in an existence form. I didn't date anybody for the whole school year.

I was very good friends with Jake, and we got together from time to time. Ironically, he had a facial tic also; and at times, I wondered if we both shared the same problem, whatever it was. I never asked him about it because I didn't want to embarrass him or hurt his feelings. I knew what it was like to be asked about something so personal and embarrassing.

In June of 1969, as my graduation day approached, I wanted to go to my senior prom. One day, when I was with Jake, I took a risk and called Danny in Florida, asking him to take me to my senior prom. To my surprise, he said yes. Just knowing that I could look forward to seeing him again, and better yet, going to the prom with him, was like being in the best dream I was ever in and not wanting to wake up for fear that it was just that, a dream.

Prom night came, and we looked pretty good, except for the wrist corsage that I had thrown in the freezer by mistake instead of the frig because I was in a hurry to do the next thing on my list before the day gave way to night. It froze, then defrosted and eventually wilted. Just as well. I would have tried to keep it for memories, and then I would have had one more thing to look back at and cry over. I wore the wrist corsage the way it was and danced at my prom as Ruby and the Romantics sang in person, "Our Day Will Come."

Instead of going to a lake the next day like everybody else was doing for the after-prom activities, Danny and I spent the next day together alone at a green grassy field where we laid out a blanket with some food I had packed. Nothing seemed to be working out. By that, I mean it was awkward being there with him because it seemed like he didn't want to be in my company. It turned out to be a big disappointment for both of us. My corsage would be a good analogy for how the day turned out and how our relationship eventually turned out that summer: It froze, then defrosted and eventually wilted. I just wanted him to love me, but I couldn't make him do that.

When Danny signed my yearbook, he said a lot of genuinely nice things and took a whole page to say them, but one thing he didn't say was that he loved me. When he went back to Florida to start his senior year, I thought it was over between us, but not yet. I still had to hang on and see if I could get this boy to love me.

After graduation, when I was working at my first real job as a clerk typist, my best friend Kristin and I started making plans to take a trip to Florida because we wanted to do something fun and we'd never flown before. I also wanted to see Danny again to try to rejuvenate our relationship, so we made reservations, and part of our trip included going to Miami Beach. When we got enough money saved, we gave notice at work and quit our jobs.

It was February of 1970. We flew to Orlando, where Danny met us at the airport. I could tell that he was glad to see me. When we got to his house in Winter Haven, I noticed some information brochures on a desk about Bible College, and his parents confirmed that Danny would be going to Bible College after he graduated. I wasn't surprised by this as we had talked about it before at his home in Stamford. Actually, he once mentioned the both of us going, which was pretty comical to me at the time, although he didn't realize it because he wasn't aware of my limitations. I'd barely gotten through high school with my sanity, so the thought of attending a four-year university and trying to compete with "smart" people was a joke to me. It's funny to me now to imagine myself at Bible College trying to find my way around on the first day, and I'm having low blood sugar and ticking so bad that people are looking at me and wondering if they should come near me or just call 911 or lay hands on me and pray. (Yes, I find this mental image hilarious, and I'm laughing my head off right now.)

I felt extremely nervous being there at his house with Kristin and both of his parents there. It was kind of like mixed company. No, it was definitely mixed company. Danny's parents were committed Christians and very nice, reserved, hard-working people with much wisdom accumulated in their years of raising six children. We were just kids trying to be grown-ups, and they probably knew it. Danny and I had some special times while there in Winter Haven, but the time flew by. And soon we were on our way to Miami. I wanted to stay in Winter Haven and try to work on my relationship with Danny, but Kristin and I stuck to our plans.

We boarded a bus and took a six-hour ride to the place we'd dreamed about for many months as we saved our money. We reached our hotel, which was right on the strip. One little problem: before we left for Miami, I'd forgotten to get traveler's checks but didn't think anything of it. Well, one thing you don't do while walking down the Miami Strip is act like a tourist. There we were with our large brim sun hats, dressed to kill, and showing off. We should have read a book on the dos and don'ts of travel rules before we left. We found some "buddies" to hang around with, or should I say, they found us. We were just young and trying to live it up and have a good time while it lasted, but unlike Kristin, I hadn't taken the money I still had left ($160) out of my wallet to put it in a safe place.

After the second night at the Fontainebleau Hotel, we got up and decided we wanted to eat breakfast outside under those big umbrellas like big shots. We ate our extravagant breakfast, and when I went to pay my bill, I discovered that all my money was gone. I had been robbed! Although we knew who had taken the money, we decided not to pursue an arrest and ruin our trip even more. So I just called my mother and asked her to wire me some money. All she could afford was $40.

We got on a Greyhound bus and headed back to Winter Haven. I was brokenhearted and feeling so bad for Kristin since I was the one who hadn't been wise in my decision-making, both in failing to get the travelers checks and not hiding my money. We must have looked pretty desperate then because a man who was eating crackers out of a box offered us some, and we partook. I had to keep by blood sugar level from dropping, so I believe now that this was God's providence. This nice man also offered us some beer, and we partook of that also because we were thirsty. (Don't know about God's providence on this one.)

We made it back to our little motel room in Winter Haven, and we survived until I could get home and pay Kristin back the money I borrowed. We did have our tickets paid both ways so we just needed money for food and the motel bill. Needless to say, our diets changed. We ate the cheapest food we could get. We were pretty depressed about all the goings-on that weren't in our plans. But even more than that, for the few days that we had left in Winter Haven before going home, Danny and I were breaking up again, and I knew that it would be a sad goodbye.

We boarded the plane, and I sat there in my seat feeling dismayed over the whole trip. I knew I was chasing an elusive dream, but I didn't want to stop. My only goal in life seemed as though I wanted to win the love of someone who couldn't nor wouldn't love me.

CHAPTER 8

Exit Six

After my costly extravaganza to Florida, I was pretty beat down. I had no job, no money, and no boyfriend. On top of that, my mother and I were moving into a house with my grandmother, who had been forced out of the only house she'd lived in for decades because a boulevard was going in. It was documented as the oldest house in Stamford's local newspaper, *The Stamford Advocate.* My uncle found a nice house for her on the west side of Stamford and purchased it.

Being a carpenter, he was able to renovate the house, and it was the nicest one I had lived in since birth. Now, for the first time in my family, there were three generations of Italian women living in the same house.

Ironically, it was very close to my old neighborhood, the Southfield Village projects I'd lived in as a child. Sadly, those four buildings were in terrible condition by then, and crime there was out of control. Looking at it from a distance not too far, I knew I would never step foot into that place again, but I also knew that the memories I'd accumulated there would walk me through any time I wanted to visit. This was where a part of my heart would always remain, even after the buildings were no longer standing. And now they are gone.

Aberdeen Street was small and quiet with lots of trees, pretty in any season. I couldn't believe that I was living in a house that was boarded with hedges. There was even a fence in the front entrance. We had an apple tree and beautiful green grass. The hedges on one side of the house offered privacy for sunbathing, and we held our annual family picnics there in the summer. Beyond the front entrance was a long foyer that led into the living room. There was a small back porch with concrete stairs. I still hold vivid memories of hallmark moments where romantic relationships either started or ended in that foyer or the back porch. This house that I would live in for such a short time was just about a block from exit six on Interstate 95, which was the exit to all the places I'd lived since I was born. Exit Six was home for me.

What I didn't know then was that my friend, Marie—from the projects, the girl that I'd played nun with—was also living on Aberdeen Street. She had moved there some time before we did. I had lost contact with her as we got older even though we'd gone to the same high school. We got reacquainted, and as time would have it, she would become a pivotal source in my very near future.

I found a new job as a teletype operator for an insurance company. I was hired as a clerk typist but soon learned that I was going to be taught how to operate a Telex and TWX machine to send information to other insurance companies. I loved this work, and the pay was good. I'd paid Kristin the money I owed her from our Florida trip, and now I had a new place to live and a nice house with all new furniture and a new job. Everything was going real good, or was it?

What was wrong was that my heart was still far away in Florida where I had apparently left it. I did stay busy at work every day as it was challenging to get all my work done while working for four underwriters. I ticked a lot from the stress of it, but no one said anything. So I just kept working. I did have a constant fear, however, that I would get called into my boss's office where he'd ask me what I was doing all the time with my head. I feared I would get fired.

Not long after getting hired, I received a phone call from Danny's brother, asking if I would like to come to the airport to pick up Danny who was flying home. Of course I said yes. I was elated and tried to look my best for him. Besides being elated, I was nervous about seeing him since I didn't know where things stood between us. When he got off the plane, it was apparent that there was still some spark left in this blond-haired, blue-eyed heartbreaker. It was the summer of 1970, and there I was, still holding on to the hope of having a future with him. But my immature, self-destructing ways would keep that from happening.

What I found shocking at that time was that he still had not said anything about my ticking, so I felt pretty sure that I'd successfully hidden it from him. I'm not saying that with a prideful attitude. I was still what-if-ing, knowing that any moment things could change instantly if I made one slipup. It was really too bad that I could exercise self-control over the tics but could not do the same with my emotional outbursts.

I don't remember what spawned this argument, but we were together with his brother sitting at a table when I remember being very upset and storming out of the place, threatening Danny that I was going to jump in a nearby body of water and kill myself. Of course, I had no intention of doing that; my only intention was to get his attention. After I gained some composure, we got into his brother's car, a luxurious black continental. He drove very fast as I cried all the way home. He got off at Exit Six and turned left, drove one block, and parked. Danny walked me into the foyer. I was crying uncontrollably by now and watching him through tear-filled eyes. He looked very upset, but considering all that had happened, he was as composed as he could be. I knew this was finally the end of our very complex long-distance, on-and-off relationship. He said good-bye and walked out the door, getting on I-95 North from Exit Six and going home with his brother. That was it. I literally cried myself to sleep that night and got up and went to work the next morning with eyes red and swollen.

Once again, my life was revolving around Exit Six, with Danny exiting my life just like my father used to do. When I was a little girl, my father, who I loved dearly at that time, would come to visit us in the projects. Sometimes when he would leave our house, he would go to his boatyard instead of going back to his house in New York. He would tell me to watch out of the kitchen window; and as soon as he got on to 1-95 from Exit Six, he would pass our window, wave, and beep the horn and go on. I would wave back to him, delighted that we had this arrangement, and I always hoped I could do it again soon. I never knew when he would be back, but I ran into his arms every time he came home. Eventually, he stopped coming.

I've learned that a little girl's relationship with her father is extremely important from the time she is born. I know that there are some fathers who have to be gone for military reasons. I also realize that some fathers have a disease or will die before their child gets to know them, and this is unfortunate. However, I am speaking here of those fathers who are living and have no reason not to be involved except by selfish motives. My father was there, in body, but his thoughts were always in other places. He was uninvolved, and I had to fight for his attention. His love was not consistent because he was gone most of the time. I know now that I was trying to satisfy a tremendous yearning that I had for my father and was seeking it in my first love. It's not meant to be that way. I know now that only my Heavenly Father can fill the void in my heart that my father left.

A father of the fatherless, a defender of wid-
ows, is God in his holy habitation. (Psalm 68:5)

45

For Dad's Only

If you are a dad and you have a daughter or may have one someday and you've read this chapter along with the last one as well, please take with all seriousness the things I've written about my longing for my earthly father and seldom having his love.

Your daughter needs exactly the same things I needed. She needs hugs and kisses early in life and special times with just the two of you to show her how special she is.

Take her on dates and show her how a man is supposed to treat a lady so she knows this before she starts dating. Don't stop hugging and kissing her because you think she is getting "too old" for this. She will never be too old to hug or kiss. Tell her often how much you love her. Play games with her. Take her for walks. Take her to the movies. Be her friend, but be her father first. You'll never regret it, and she'll never forget it. I promise you this.

CHAPTER 9

Please Don't Love Me

I've been at my new job for a few months now. You'll recall that I was hired as a clerk typist but actually got trained to use a TWX and Telex machine. I thought it was a miracle that I even got hired. It was always nerve-racking to go in for an interview knowing that I'd tic and not know if I'd be fired the first time someone caught me doing this. I never knew whether I should put on the application form that I had diabetes because I thought it would be a strike against me for getting hired.

This job had more challenges and responsibilities than I'd anticipated. I was in a more open space than my last job, and everybody could see me as I worked in my open cubicle. I enjoyed this job, and the pay was better. If only I could quit ticking, but I knew that wasn't going to happen. Sometimes I would work overtime and get home very late and eat dinner that my mother kept warm in the oven. Marie would come by and visit, but I would be so tired after working that I did not have any energy to talk much. I just wanted to go to bed. By now, Marie was married to a sailor who was stationed in Dam Neck, Virginia. She hadn't moved down to live there with her husband yet. She wondered if I would mind going out with one of her husband's friends, a sailor himself. I said okay, but without much interest.

It wasn't long before I got a letter from him. We began corresponding regularly, and he seemed very nice, even though he couldn't spell to save his life. But being a good speller, I could usually figure out most of what he was saying. We were planning to meet soon.

We had our first phone call to hear each other's voices and to do the compare-and-contrast thing by asking stupid questions such as, "Do you smoke?"

"Smoke what?" he said.

To which I answered, "Cigarettes," wondering why he would think that I was suggesting anything else. As it turned out, we both did smoke cigarettes. Both our mothers' names were Joyce, and both of them had four children. He was from a place called Sweet Home, Oregon, and he had a mild accent that seemed countryish to me. His name was Lester Marion Stoddard.

The letter writing and the first phone call led to the first visit. He promised he would never come to visit unannounced, but that's exactly what he did, having to catch a ride with Marie and her husband whenever they were coming, but I still thought he could have called and said he was on his way.

It was Thanksgiving 1970, and I had my hair rolled up in large pink and lavender rollers since I was getting ready to go to my uncle's house for a traditional Italian-style Thanksgiving dinner. Then I heard a loud knock on the door followed by Marie yelling, "Faith, Lester's here. Lester's here!"

It couldn't be, but it was. I tore the rollers out of my hair so fast that I was pulling hair out with them. I ran the brush through my half-wet hair real fast, and then there he was, with just that much warning. I greeted him with a kiss on the cheek and did the same to Marie and her husband as this was a custom of sorts in New England among Italian people. The next four days that he was there were a blur, except for one of the nights when he was walking me into my house to say goodbye for the night. We had our first kiss right there on my back porch, and it was sweet. I had the feeling that he liked me very much. I came in the house and asked my mother the question I always asked after returning home. "Did anybody call?"

"Yes," she said, "somebody called, but I don't want to tell you who." That gave it away because I knew it was Danny. Apparently, he was home on a Thanksgiving break. I never returned his call. I was finally moving on.

As the summer months passed and fall was beginning to turn rapidly into winter, I began to experience a very unusual fear and anxiety that started out of nowhere. This time, the fear was the first of its kind. I had this fear that I would hear voices in my head for some reason, and it began to infiltrate every part of my life so much that I was afraid to be alone. I became severely depressed, but at the same time, I was going to work and working overtime and trying to keep a stiff upper lip. I didn't let anybody know what was going on inside my head, not even my mother this time. I couldn't shake this thing no matter what. Between the fear and the depression combined, I thought I would go crazy. I started taking Valium again and kept refilling the prescription. Back then, Valium was the drug of choice for anxiety, but oh, how addictive it was.

For Christmas, Lester flew home to California to see his mother and to officially break up with his former girlfriend. He then flew to JFK to come and be with me for the New Year. I was so messed up mentally that I made up an excuse to Marie and her husband for why I couldn't go to the airport with them to pick him up. I felt so guilty, but I was more sick than guilty. When we were together again, he gave me a Christmas gift. It was in a ring box. *That was not good*, I thought. I was exceedingly riddled with fear as I opened the gift, but it turned out to be a very beautiful garnet ring. My birthday is in January, so it was the perfect gift. I was so relieved! My gift to him was a very attractive silver butane cigarette lighter. He liked it and used it for a short time. It was too nice to use every day, he said.

Marie's sister was giving a New Year's Eve party, and Lester and I were invited. I remember two unexpected things that happened that night while at the party. We got snowed in because of a blizzard and had to spend the night. The other thing was more troubling. Lester made it known to me that he wanted to get married. Now there I was, carrying around baggage that he didn't even know about, and I wasn't about to tell him when I didn't even know the name for what I had, except to call it "severe mental problems." And then there was the ticking and the diabetes. How could I get married? What I

49

needed was a shrink, not a husband, but I couldn't afford a shrink. Lester didn't know about the Valium either. What a mess I was in!

When the holidays were over, Lester returned to Virginia, and I returned to work but felt a mental collapse waiting in the wings. It amazes me now to think back on those days and see how God's hand was on me even though I didn't know it then. My job did keep me very busy with trying to keep insurance underwriters happy, which meant keeping my inbox clear. Overtime became a way of life, but walking in the dark to catch a bus was not my cup of tea. I looked forward to Lester's next visit home, but that wouldn't be for at least another one and a half months. Valium was becoming my friend, but it would prove to be a very deceiving enemy in the end.

Valentine's Day was approaching, and Lester was on his way to Connecticut. I was looking forward to seeing him. He brought with him a special gift of course since he was going to be here for Valentine's Day. But he didn't wait for Valentine's Day to give it to me. We were alone, and it was 2:00 a.m. when he said to me, "If you're ever going to leave me, do it now." Right after that, he pulled a diamond ring out of his shirt pocket and placed it on my finger. Suddenly I was engaged to be married to this sailor who would make any woman the happiest in the world, but he wanted me. I felt so guilty for not being overjoyed, but I was so preoccupied with mental issues that were tormenting me that I couldn't even feel joy when I should have.

When you're dealing with an undiagnosed illness, it can rob you of your very life. Certainly it robbed me of feeling the joy and delight of having a truly unique man love me and the joy of all the special moments like getting engaged. It was doing just that to me (stealing my sanity), and I was bringing this wonderful man into my life—a man who was totally innocent, sweet, sound in body and mind, and one who didn't deserve the trouble that I would bring upon him as his wife if I didn't straighten out. And I didn't. I just couldn't.

In March of 1971, Lester got stationed in Groton, Connecticut. That made things so much better because now we were only two and a half hours apart, and he usually rented or borrowed a car and drove down to Stamford on Friday nights and went back on Sunday. He wanted me to meet his family in Santa Ana, California; so when the month of May came, he took out a loan and bought two round-trip tickets to LAX and a beautiful set of Samsonite luggage for me, and we flew to Los Angeles. I took my Valium with me. I never left home without it.

CHAPTER 10

California

I don't remember the flight at all, and I wish I couldn't remember this particular trip. But I do remember, and I am going to tell in detail as much as I can about what was going through my mind because it is imperative that whoever reads this understands that I did live through this.

I still find it unbelievable that Lester could not see by now that something wasn't right about me. I was ticking so much that I thought for sure that he would finally ask me what was wrong with me, just like I feared with Danny. I was very fearful of meeting his mom and the rest of the family too but especially his mom since I knew she would be studying me thoroughly as her future daughter-in-law. I didn't get introduced to her in the usual way. It happened as Lester and I were walking down a street in his mom's neighborhood, and suddenly there was his family, passing us in a car. They stopped, and we both got in. I got in the back seat, and there we met. Nobody talked fast or used their hands to talk or yelled to get a point across. I knew one thing for sure; there was no Italian blood in these people, but that was okay. I also learned that only one plate is used for eating a meal, unlike having a separate plate for salad and roll, like we did on the East Coast. But I figured I could live with that.

Lester's mom gave me her bedroom to sleep in while I was there. It was off the main house with another bedroom. Her brother, Bill, lived with her. He was very quiet but pleasant. Lester has three siblings, his brother, sixteen at the time, and two older sisters.

It didn't take long to see that I was liked by his family. This fact made me uneasy because I knew that I had issues that needed attention, and I wasn't sure how long I could go on without them becoming suspicious. I was alone in my secret about being mentally unstable, and now I had added to the list all these wonderful people who thought everything was normal with me. For the most part, I was acting normal, joking, playing around with Lester like engaged couples do, cleaning up dishes, and conversing with his family; but inside, I was fighting between what is reality and what is not. By that, I mean that I knew where I was and who I was with and why I was there; but at the same time, my mind was at war with itself, fighting against what I can only call the most severe case of anxiety I'd ever had, one that was mixed with depression, fear, and confusion.

I thought that I was literally going to be scared to death or go insane. My ticking could serve as an outward appearance of what was going on inside me at that time, and I was so glad I'd taken Valium with me. But as bad as I felt, there were still times when I felt almost sane and normal. It just didn't last very long.

Some of those times, I felt were times that I know now that God had provided for me. For instance, Lester's mother, and his brother as well, can play the guitar. One night, as I was listening to his mom play, very quietly strumming a song, my body began to relax. I could feel myself just unwind, and I felt at peace. What a wonderful feeling it was to know that there was something that could make me calm down, even if only for a few moments. His brother's playing and singing had the same effect on me. I know now that these were blessings provided by God as He was carrying me through this journey, one I was living minute by minute, never knowing what was around the corner. God's Word says, "For we walk by faith, not by sight" (2 Corinthians 5:7). But at this time in my life, I was not walking by faith. My Valium was the only thing in my sight, and that's what my faith was in.

One night, we all went out, and I remember being in a room with a pool table. Lester's mom and his brother were there. All of a sudden, I started getting the urge to say things, but not out loud. Instead, I was saying them to myself, in my mind, and they were things that were awful. For example, I'd say to myself, "She's as dumb as they come," only I didn't mean it. I just had to repeat it in my mind. So this was one more explosive surprise that came out of nowhere, and I had to deal with it.

When I look back now at the events that took place after my trip to Florida, I see that it was quite a ride, to say the least. First, the breakup with my high school sweetheart, then the move, the new job, and the fear of hearing voices settling in like a comfortable cat on a windowsill in the afternoon sun, then meeting Lester, getting engaged, and quitting my job to come to California. And there I was, in the state of California and pretty much in a state of misery. I just wanted to go home or wake up from an exceptionally long, bad dream, like Dorothy in *The Wizard of Oz*. It doesn't seem fair that I was not enjoying this time in my life to the fullest like every other girl who gets engaged. I had a sweet fiancé who loved me and was the most wonderful man I'd ever met, who took me all the way to California to meet his family and more; but I was feeling too sick to care, appreciate, and enjoy this special time in my life. I was running on empty.

I look back sometimes and wish things had not happened the way they did. That is not to say that God wasn't with me through all of it. What I should have done when I started having the fear of hearing voices was get some help and find out why this was happening and get a diagnosis, if possible. I would have been on some kind of controlled prescription or maybe some psychotherapy to delve into my symptoms including the ticking and the obsessive-compulsive behavior.

I often ask myself why I didn't do things differently, such as tell somebody what I was going through, but I still don't know who that would have been. I always held things in until I just couldn't hold them anymore. It's kind of like getting sick to your stomach and wanting to throw up, but hating to do it. Then all of a sudden, you're going to pass out, but you throw up instead. Well, I was still in that "sick to my stomach" stage, where I thought I would remain indefinitely.

Going North

Lester wanted me to meet his dad in Vancouver, Washington, but first to visit some of his friends from his hometown in Sweet Home, Oregon. Then we were planning on going all the way up to Fort Lewis, Washington, to see his other sister. We didn't have a car, so Lester went to a car lot close to his mother's house and picked out a car, put a sizeable down payment on it, and drove it off the lot.

Before we left on this road trip, he told his mom what he'd done, saying that he'd put the car in her name and that when we got back, the car was hers, and she could pay it off. She was just fine with it, and that let me know that there was a special relationship between them. She trusted anything Lester did and did not question him. He knew about cars to a great extent, so he knew this one would run for a long time before he even decided to put it in her name. So off we went to Sweet Home, Oregon.

The drive was very long, and I still didn't know a lot about this man I was engaged to. I found out that he didn't pack for a trip until he was ready to go. Then he just threw clothes in a box and was packed. I wished I could be like that, but even as bad as I felt, I had to pack everything just so. I hated living out of a suitcase, and I just wanted to take a bath or shower. But they were few and far between on this trip.

The closer we got to our destination, the more anxious and sicker I felt inside. The voices fear was driving me crazy, and the silence in the car was getting the best of me. I kept flipping through the radio stations but couldn't get much as we were going through mountain ranges for most of the trip. Back then, there were no CDs, iPods, or even cassette tapes, just the radio. I managed to sleep on and off, and I never drove. I didn't have a license. I could have not driven in the state of mind I was in anyway.

We got to Sweet Home, and it was time to get out and meet some people. Just what I needed! Upon entering the house, I knew these were countrypeople. They were friends that Lester had gone to school with and grown up with all his life. They were the come-on-in-and-grab-a-beer kind of folk. The house was old, big, dark, and gloomy. I wanted to get out of there and run home, but instead I asked if I could lie down. And that's where I stayed much of the time I was there. I cried in an old squeaky bed, and it was all I could do. Occasionally, Lester would come in and check on me and give me a hug, then go back to his friends. Didn't he realize that something wasn't quite right with me? I wondered why he wasn't asking me questions about my behavior.

I was not taking care of my diabetes, so I knew my blood sugar was out of control. I knew I was losing weight too, but I felt that was the least of my problems for the time being. What was really bothering me was how I was going to marry this man, have children, and live a normal life. This seemed like an impossible thing to even consider. How could I have kids when I couldn't even take care of myself? I felt like a total failure.

The thought of suicide never entered my mind through this time in my life or any other time before it which I am humbly grateful for. God's Word, the Bible says, "Or do you not know that your body is the temple of the Holy Spirit who is in you, whom you have from God, and you are not your own? For you were bought at a price; therefore, glorify God in your body and in your spirit, which are God's" (1 Corinthians 6:19–20). This tells me now that it is not an option to take my own life without facing eternal judgment. That price talked about in the Bible is the blood of Jesus Christ, God's only begotten son. He died in our place so we would not have to die eternally in our sin. I am glad I have this knowledge now because I know that I should not take my own life regardless of how bad things might get. I know that God and only God is the one who will judge all men. But I am not so close-minded as to think that some people who may have committed suicide will necessarily go to hell. I leave that up to God. Only He knows each situation.

There are questions in this lifetime that I will never get the answer to on this side of heaven. I am trying to be more accepting of this fact because I want to be able to put those unanswered questions at rest and know that whenever I need an answer to a "why, God" question, that He will either give me one or I don't need to know and should therefore trust Him. I believe that the answer to all our questions is in God's Word. That doesn't necessarily mean that we will find a particular answer to a particular question all the time, but it does mean that if we study God's Word thoroughly and learn of God's personality through both the old and new testament, that we may have less of those "why, God" questions because we will know more of who God is. "For my thoughts are not your thoughts, nor are your ways My ways, says the Lord" (Isaiah 55:8). This scripture gives us even more reason to trust His supernatural ability to be in total control even when we don't think He has total control of our deepest darkness.

My earthly father was a fisherman on the Long Island Sound for a good part of his years. I enjoyed it immensely whenever he took me out in his motorboat across the Long Island Sound, and I never experienced any fear or danger while with him. That was because he was my father, and no matter what, I believed he would protect me. One time, we hit some big waves, and the boat started to take on water. He had some coffee cans on hand, and he told me to fill them with water and throw it over the boat. I just kept doing that until there was no more water in the boat. He instructed until there was no more water in the boat. I never gave it any thought that I would drown or otherwise be harmed. I trusted my earthly father to protect me, and that is all there was to it. So why is it harder to sometimes trust our Heavenly Father less than we trust our earthly father?

We continued our trip up north to see my future father-in-law in the Portland/Vancouver area. Our first stop was Great-Aunt Lucy's house. I got acquainted with Aunt Lucy. She was a little old lady with spunk and a big heart. She had diabetes also. Lester's dad was a short and stocky man with a flattop; and he was a nice, respectful person who loved the outdoors. In his earlier days, he hunted and fished a lot with his two sons and was a natural with a gun. In fact, he took us practice shooting. I had never had a real gun in my hand before, but there I was—an unstable, frightened, and insecure basket case who was about to shoot at heads and chests on paper targets. So I did. It was very loud and unnerving, the last thing I needed, of course.

The sleeping arrangements were that the women stayed with the women and the men stayed with the men. Lester went home with his dad, and I slept at Aunt Lucy's house. I had been trying to ration out my Valium because it was still a little over a week before I would be back in Connecticut, so I hadn't taken any for about two days. And I could tell, of course, because the voices fear was closing in on me like the feds on Bonnie and Clyde just before they were gunned down.

The bedroom furniture was old, of course, with doilies under everything. The house was damp, cool, and it was raining outside. I could hear the rain on the windows and a clock in the distance, ticking as I lay there not moving, eyes wide open, body stiff, and full of anxious fear, waiting for the voices to start at any time. I lay there, unable to do anything to remedy the dire situation I was in, thinking, "I'll go crazy before morning." The silence was my enemy now, and all I could do was lie there and wait for this overwhelming paralyzing fear to go away. Morning finally came, and Aunt Lucy peeked into my room and asked me if I wanted breakfast. I told her that I wanted to sleep a little longer.

As I settled in at Aunt Lucy's for another night, she wanted to show me some old photo albums. Well, as she was flipping through the pages and talking to me, it started again. No, not the fear, but the feeling of calmness that began to go through my body just like the time when Lester's mom and brother played their guitars. There was something about looking at the photo albums and listening to Aunt Lucy's voice that settled me, and I began to relax for the first time without any problem. I know now that God intervened and put me at rest once again. It's one thing to fall into a restful sleep. It is another thing to fight all night with your fear and finally "pass out" in bed until you wake up. Someone was praying for me. I still relive that night, now fifty years ago.

After another three hours on the road, we reached Fort. Lewis, Washington, where Lester's sister lived. Our visit there was very short. Lester's sister and her family did not have much in the way of material things, and I got the impression that she was struggling with life and later learned that she was. I told myself that I would never live on the West Coast, especially the Northwest, and never live on a military base either. Did somebody say never say never?

Detour

As I began to observe, Lester was in his own world (a normal one), and I was in mine. Well okay, he was in mine too, but only by what I verbalized to him in our conversations. I must have been the most boring person in womankind. Things did get pretty intense when we had a certain conversation before leaving Oregon. He wanted to marry me before we went back to California—in other words, elope in Vegas. He was going to Scotland as soon as we got back to Connecticut and wanted me to have the ring on my finger then. He also said that my allotment check could start coming while he was away, which was going to be for a year and a half.

Let's see, as I saw it then, I'd be secretly married, unemployed, and without a husband for eighteen months. Going home wasn't sounding so good anymore. I would have to face these issues and deal with them, including my mental status. How did things get so out of hand? I agreed with his decision to get married before going back to California, but this would put us on the road longer. And we were worried that his family might become suspicious or fear that we had an accident.

We didn't just breezily drive to Vegas and take our vows and leave as we had planned. No. Lester got on a wrong highway that led us so far from our destination that we actually went back just a little ways into California and then back east toward what we hoped was Nevada. Then he realized that we were closer to Reno than Vegas, so we aimed to get married in Reno. But by the time we got there, it was too late in the evening, so we had no choice but to keep moving as we would waste time just sitting and waiting. So we headed for Vegas once again.

You can't make this stuff up. There was one time during our quest to find a Justice of the Peace that we ended up driving where there was snow on the ground. Lester stopped the car, and I woke up in the back seat and turned to look for him. And he was outside the car, filling my insulin thermos with ice to keep it cold. It was nearing the end of the month of May, so we had to be in some mountain range to see snow. It definitely wasn't the Vegas strip.

After driving for hours, we were hot, tired, and dirty and wanted to get cleaned up. We did, but not in the conventional way. There was nothing conventional about this trip or the man I was about to marry. We pulled into a gas station very close to the town hall building in Vegas. We used the bathrooms to get cleaned up. I ran water in the tiniest sink I'd ever seen, took soap out of my suitcase, and had a spit bath with cold water. I brushed my teeth and put on fresh makeup and slapped a blond wig on over my black hair, and there you have it. I couldn't believe I'd done what I just did, but there we were, all spiffed up in our wedding duds. I wore some very heavy gray and white pants with a long sleeveless vest and a long-sleeved shirt underneath. Lester wore a pink pinstriped, short-sleeved shirt with green pants and cowboy boots. No bouquet, no boutonniere, no bridesmaids, no best man, no white wedding gown, no, it was just us, doing something most people plan for months, even years.

It was May 28, 1971, and we had just tied the knot. We were husband and wife. At this point, I had very mixed emotions. I had an excitement in me for getting married, but my mental situation hadn't gone away just because I'd taken my wedding vows. And I knew it wouldn't. I had no appetite as we sat there at IHOP. I can't remember what I ate. All I could think of was, *This is not the way you're supposed to feel on your wedding day.*

While driving through the desert, I saw tumbleweed for the first time. I had never seen it before this trip to California. Tumbleweed gets its name from the branching upper part of various plants which become detached from the roots and succumb to the wind wherever it blows. The more I thought about it, the more I began to see myself as a piece of tumbleweed. At some time in my past, I had become detached from life itself as I used to know it when I was a child. Since then, I had been moving in some direction, but not necessarily one of my own because I had become unable to do so without the help of others. I was detached from reality much like tumbleweed becomes detached from its roots. And when one feels detached from reality, they are detached from their very heart, mind, body, and strength.

CHAPTER 11

Coming Home, Then
Going Home

I didn't realize how stressful it would be to come back home to Connecticut. It was as if I was going from one bad dream to another in the same night without waking up. In just three days, Lester was gone; and having to say goodbye after spending almost every waking hour with him for almost a month and being married to him now but not able to tell anybody was enough for my heart to explode.

The weight of the trip was lying heavily on me. A feeling of total displacement and emptiness had taken over now that he was gone. For so long, I'd held so much in that I couldn't just grab a family member or a friend and say, "Look, I need someone to talk to." After all, where would I start? Besides that, once they learned that I was married after a lengthy, leisurely trip to California with my fiancé, why should I have any problems? No, there was not one person I could think of who would be able to understand all I had gone through and then help me. I figured that was for a psychiatrist to try to sort out, but I didn't have any money for one. I did contact the local hospital where I used to go to for diabetic checkups where they knew me very well.

I got evaluated for intensity of my problem, and they felt it was good to put me in a group therapy session. I thought for sure that they would put me with a psychiatrist with one-on-one counseling, but they didn't. The cost was very little or nothing, and that's just what I got out of it. I found that I could not open up to the people in the group. My issues seemed to be too complicated to share with people I didn't know or trust. After a few weeks or so, I quit.

There was now a slight chance that I could have been pregnant, but I wasn't—and that was a good thing. But I had lost ten pounds from all the stress, plus not eating right. I was probably spilling ketones in my urine, which is very bad for a diabetic, and that could have attributed to the weight loss. This was weight I could not afford to lose.

Scar Tissue

As I write this book, I am currently receiving physical therapy treatments two times a week for surgery that I had on my right shoulder and elbow. It has been five weeks since the surgery, and I am still in pain and cannot fully use my right arm yet. Scar tissue builds up after surgery, and it literally has to be broken up, but not without enduring a great amount of pain. The physical therapist stretches and massages the parts of my arm where the scar tissue is. She also very carefully positions my arm and shoulder and moves it more and more in the direction it doesn't want to go until I give her the "funny look" that lets her know I can't tolerate any more pain, so she stops moving it. She does this over and over until my time is up. She keeps doing this procedure every time I come in and will continue to do it until I get my full range of motion back.

I'm not a stranger to physical therapy, as I had the same operation in 1992 on my left shoulder. So there lies the hope that I will fully recover as I did in 1992. So why did I say all this? As I was working out on my treadmill the other day, I thought about the term *scar tissue*. I have a lot of visible scars on my body from different surgeries, from hot oil splashing on me while cooking, a cut here or there that didn't heal right, biopsies, trigger finger releases, etc. These scars are visible, and if and when I happen to look at them, my memory naturally goes back to the day I got that particular scar and why. While some scars can be seen on the outside of the body, scar tissue is often inside the body also. As I mentioned, breaking up scar tissue is a very painful process but necessary to reach optimum recovery.

You've probably figured out by now that we don't get to choose what life will bring our way. I did not choose Tourette's syndrome, depression, obsessive thoughts, or type 1 diabetes. These things, along with other life issues discussed in this book, have left unpleasant and sometimes debilitating memories or what I call "scar tissue." I know that just because I have this "scar tissue," I must not just quit and sit down and lick my wounds. That's not what God would want me to do. Instead, I have to exercise my will to go on and live my life in spite of the pain I may feel, or I will cease to function as a human being, a child of God with real purpose in life. Likewise, if I quit my physical therapy in midstream, I can expect to lose proper function of my right arm. I would not be able to iron clothes, work in my garden, fix my hair, paint a room, or hug my grandchildren real tight, along with many other things that I like to do.

In the end, it becomes a matter of the will to keep breaking up "scar tissue" that is bound to form in everyone's life. This is not easy to do, but it is possible because God made a way through Jesus Christ. In 2 Corinthians 12:7–8, the apostle Paul speaks of a thorn in his flesh, a messenger of Satan, to keep him from becoming conceited. Paul pleads with the Lord three times to remove it from him, but the Lord says to him, "My grace is sufficient for you, for my strength is made perfect in weakness" (2 Corinthians 12:9).

If God's grace was great enough for Paul and gave him perfect strength in his weakness, then it is great enough for you and me. I immediately thought of this verse from the Old Testament that supports 2 Corinthians 12:19, "When the enemy comes in like a flood, the Spirit of the Lord will lift up a standard against him" (Isaiah 59:19). I wish I'd known that Satan was my enemy back when I was literally in fear of losing my sanity. I knew about God and Jesus and that God was my heavenly father and that Jesus died on the cross for me, but I had not yet personalized this fact in my heart. Yet it is apparent that God was with me through the whole trip to California and had brought me safely home. My mother's prayers for me were being heard too, and God was intervening on her behalf.

I did not know it then, but God was working out something of a miracle that neither my husband nor I could have imagined. It was still June, and I was settled in and wondering what I would do for eighteen months without seeing Lester. I finally got up the nerve to tell my mother that I was married. She seemed pleased and acted like she already knew about it, even though she couldn't have. I eventually told my sister and brother. We still had intentions of having a big wedding in a church with all the trimmings, and because of that, we didn't tell his family about our eloping. In the meantime, I was going to be in a wedding in September.

I have a cousin on my mother's side of whose name is Theresa. We have been very close since our childhood because we got type 1 diabetes just six months apart from each other. Needless to say, we buddied up and spent lots of time together in our teens. We could always make each other laugh, and we still do. Just before my trip to California, she asked me to be her maid of honor in her wedding. Of course, I accepted, but I was wondering all the time why she picked me above all of her close school friends because she knew that I had a nervous twitch and that her getting married in a big Catholic church with lots of guests could exacerbate my twitching symptoms. I worried that I wouldn't be able to keep my head still long enough to get through the ceremony. Frankly, the thought of going into twitch mode while standing at the altar, where the whole church could see, terrified me. I didn't want to embarrass her or myself for that matter.

Well, the day came, and the ceremony went very smooth. I managed to control the ticking. Besides that, all eyes were on the bride, not me. The reception was fun with music and dancing, and I was feeling good for a change, and for the first time in months. I didn't tell Theresa that I had eloped in May until she was married for a few months, and even then, it was over the phone. For some reason, I was scared that she would be upset with me; but of course, she wasn't. She just wondered why I had not told her sooner.

Honey, I'm Home

Remember when I said earlier about God working something out? Well, let me tell you what He did. Of course, if you're a skeptic or don't believe in God, I can understand why you may say, "Oh, things like that always happen." And maybe they do, but I believe that nothing happens without God's knowledge and His allowance of it, whether good or bad.

I was not home at the time, but my mother got a phone call from Lester, telling her that he was in Charleston, South Carolina. She quickly tracked me down and told me the breaking news over the phone, and in five days, I was packed and flying to where he was, where he had already set up house in a single-wide trailer. Here's what God did to make that happen.

Les had flown over to Holy Loch, Scotland, and reported to the USS Canopus (a submarine tender) just like he was supposed to. His orders were to be on the tender for eighteen months, which was a bit too long for us to go without seeing each other, especially since we had married just days before he left. Because of this, he volunteered for submarines with the hopes of getting assigned to one that would get him back to the States a lot sooner. It turned out that there was an opening on the USS Daniel Boone, which was coming back from patrol. The home port for the Daniel Boone is Charleston, South Carolina, so he made his first patrol with the gold crew while the blue crew flew to Charleston for their turn for shore duty.

After three months, it was the gold crew's turn to come home to Charleston. That put Lester back in the States in October of 1971, just four months from the first time he left for Scotland. The mobile home he rented for us belonged to a sailor from the blue crew, so he had already worked that out with the owner before he flew back to Charleston. When I stepped off the plane, he was there to meet me, and it was so good to see him again. This was the first place we lived as man and wife. This tiny suburb of Charleston was called Goose Creek. We celebrated our first Christmas in that single-wide mobile home. It was a no-frills kind of Christmas, but we were just happy to be together again.

I don't know what would have come of the both of us if we'd had to wait eighteen months before we saw each other again; but when I entertain my thoughts about it now, I dare say that our marriage, which had barely started (seven days total), would have not survived. How much can a newly married man, twenty years of age, tolerate without his wife before he starts to fall into temptation? Besides that, my mental condition was very unstable, and I was vulnerable to doing anything it took to make myself feel like a human being again. There is no telling what I might have done, but it would have been of no benefit to our marriage. But God knew our circumstances and intervened as He always does, usually right before we think we can't go another step.

I wish now that I'd known that then. And yes, even now, fifty years later, I still forget that God is sovereign and will take care of matters that are out of my hands. What is important is that He doesn't forget me in my human state. He knows that I will fall flat on my face again, but He will pick me up every single time.

CHAPTER 12

Charleston: The Good, the Bad, and the Ugly

Before I even flew to South Carolina, I had one very important thing that I had to get done. I was told by my doctor that, as a type 1 diabetic, I should not risk getting pregnant, so it was imperative that I had a form of birth control before I left. That doctor, who had taken care of me ever since I became a diabetic, suggested an intrauterine device be implanted in me. It was one that started being used in the midsixties called the (Saf-T-Coil). I seem to remember being told that it had only a 1 percent pregnancy rate, which made me feel pretty secure about not becoming pregnant. I wasn't ready for children then and wasn't sure I ever would be. With the IUD implanted, I felt pretty safe.

Charleston was our home for almost three years, from September of 1971 through June of 1974. Some very memorable things took place in those three years. But I still had my mental issues with irrational fear, anxiety, depression, along with the head ticking. The worst times I can remember regarding my illness were actually produced by my own irrational thoughts and fears. It was that my particular category of irrational thoughts themselves couldn't be compared with the regular things that people thought of or suffered through, and it made my stomach do flips because I realized it was outside of ordinary.

This began to interrupt my sleep. Yet I managed to act and feel normal on the outside except for the ticking, of course. That pit in the bottom of my stomach or the feeling of my stomach dropping was that same feeling I'd lived with almost constantly in California and Connecticut when it all started in the fall of 1970 (except for the ticking and facial grimaces which began when I was a child). It is like getting the worst news you can imagine or seeing a ghost that nobody else sees. You shake inside because you're scared, but nobody else knows what's going on.

Yet at times, I managed to even feel somewhat normal, such as when I was in the company of five or six other couples around somebody's kitchen table playing cards for hours. I'd have so much fun, feeling as though all my mental issues were taking a vacation, but they always greeted me with a giant hello after the fun was over. Those vacations did for me what vacations are supposed to do. They gave me a small break from the daily chaos of the life in my mind. They were a *godsend* in every sense of the word. I had quite a sense of humor then, and I still do. That was the one positive God-given gift that made it easier for me to cope with myself and be liked by other people. It served me well in those days and even more so today.

Submariners (my husband being one of them) are quite special people. They are tough but know how to live each day to the fullest without worrying about the day they have to say goodbye once again to their families and go out to sea for another two and a half months. They live in the moment, and they do it well.

There was nothing more exciting or rewarding than the day the guys were flying home and my girlfriends and I would dress up in our finest and look as beautiful as Maybelline would let us, and we'd drive out to the airport where we would wait and finally get to watch the chartered jet full of submariners coming in for a landing. Then the long wait while they all go through customs and finally looking for your special one, teary-eyed, you spot him, and he spots you. And it's heaven on earth again, at least for a while.

Remember, there were no cell phones, computers, e-mail, web-cams, Skype, or texting in the seventies. When you said goodbye, it was, "Goodbye until I see you again and hear your lovely voice. I love you."

With a large bonus for shipping over, we bought our first house and our first new car. We already had an old sixty-something, four-cylinder, four-door, stick shift blue Datsun that we bought from one of his Navy friends, but it was not driver-friendly. Our new car was a yellow 1972 Ford Torino Sport. Lester was teaching me how to drive with both cars, but it soon became apparent that I needed to have a real instructor with a lot of patience if I was to get my license. It became obvious that both of us would be safer if I went to driving school.

It was about that time that I developed a pilonidal cyst, and halfway through my lessons, I had to have emergency surgery to have it removed. This took two months to heal, during which time it was very painful to sit down. I resumed my driving lessons afterward and got my driver's license. It wasn't without a few big mess ups, but I managed to keep from ticking throughout all the lessons (and there were many). By now, Lester was out to sea, and I had a brand-new car and a license but was afraid to drive by myself. I had to force myself to go places just to get used to driving alone. It was a great accomplishment for me to get my driver's license simply because I didn't think I could actually pull it off. I give God the credit for getting my driver's license because it was a miracle.

What I am about to tell you next is something in which I did not see the hand of God until many years later. It was November 1973, and we were still living in Charleston, South Carolina. I noticed that I was sleeping during the day and feeling sluggish, dizzy, and nauseous most of the time. I didn't feel like cooking and would gag at the thought of spaghetti sauce.

That's when I knew I had to be pregnant. The same thing had happened to my sister. But I thought I could not get pregnant with the IUD device implanted with just a 1 percent chance of pregnancy. After I got tested and it came back positive, there was no question about it. I was pregnant!

I was excited and scared and worried. I had no knowledge at that time of why diabetics should not get pregnant, so when I told

Lester that night, we were happy about the news and decided to make the best of the situation. I was scheduled to attend an all-day introduction class about my pregnancy and to see my doctor. I received instruction on how to hold, bathe, change, and feed a baby, along with other related things. It was the doctor visit and what he told me that had me crying as I drove home that night. The Navy doctor I was assigned to had the audacity to tell me that I had only a 40 percent chance of giving birth to my baby. In other words, he was saying that I would probably have a miscarriage or deliver an unhealthy baby.

I realize now that he was giving me a statistical fact, but it was the derogatory nature in which he said it that I took notice of. Then he scolded me for getting pregnant in the first place. Needless to say, I was very hurt and discouraged, as well as shocked by his insensitive, unfriendly bedside manner. I wondered why any ob-gyn doctor would tell someone who is pregnant such discouraging odds even if they were true.

Also, since he knew the odds were against me because of the diabetes, didn't he know that I would get upset and that this could raise my blood sugar, which would be the worst thing for me and the baby? I was by myself here, and I felt defenseless against his assumption that I had done this purposely, as if I was some irresponsible, uncaring person. With tears flowing down my cheeks, I could hardly see in front of me as I drove home that late afternoon. In January, I began to spot, so I was scheduled to get admitted in the hospital to get my blood sugar regulated with the idea that this would help the pregnancy along. Because there still was no real accurate way of testing blood glucose, I never knew if my blood sugar was too low unless I felt the symptoms. Like all the other diabetics at that time, I was still using the urine and test tube method. Since then, we have made milestones in accuracy testing and in all other aspects of diabetes, for which I am very grateful for today.

On January 29, 1974, Lester brought me to the newly built Navy hospital where I got a private room and settled in. I was still spotting, but I had no cramps and was not very concerned with my situation. Later that night, a nurse came in and gave me a pill which

I took with a glass of water. She then pulled up a chair and began talking to me. I wasn't quite sure of her intentions. I only remember part of a phrase that she uttered to me, and it was this, "Sometimes things just don't work out." The rest of the phrase was fuzzy. She then got up and left. After that, I began having to empty my bladder about every ten minutes or so. Then it was about the fifth time when I sat down on the toilet that I felt my baby drop out of my body into the toilet water. I knew what it was because I could see plainly that it was flesh-colored, and there was no blood at all. I screamed and went into the hallway and got the attention of the nurse (the same one who had been sitting in the chair in my room), and she came running from the hallway into my room and then grabbed the flesh that was lying on the bottom of the toilet and ran out of my room and down the hall with her hand in a fist. That was the last time I saw my ten-week-old fetus and the last time I saw her.

My doctor was not on call that night, but a decision was made to take out the IUD. I was horror stricken by now and lying on a gurney in the middle of a hallway, screaming in pain and also for my husband, while some doctor was pulling at the IUD, trying to get it out. My husband got there as soon as he could, and by then, I was back in my room. And they had me hooked up to a Pitocin drip that was set on high to contract my uterus to rid myself of the afterbirth. I was having contractions every three to five minutes and screaming with every one of them. I was also bleeding profusely. Lester was trying to comfort me and at the same time wondering why this had happened. He was so hurt watching me suffer but unable to do anything except hold my hand and talk to me. He told me later that I was raising my body off the bed by two feet every time I had a contraction. I was so thirsty, but I was told I couldn't have any water at all. And Lester was only allowed to stay for one hour.

He left about 1:00 a.m. I begged them to let him stay longer, but they wouldn't allow it. The contractions, the screaming, and the bleeding went on until 6:00 a.m. Then it all ended. I was finally quiet, but I had no strength to even talk. I noticed that I was as white as a sheet when I got a chance to look in a mirror as I was sitting in my wheelchair waiting to have lung x-rays before going to have a D&C. I went home the next day and resumed my life. I had no complications.

Did God know that this was going to happen? Of course He did. He's omniscient. Could God have kept this from happening? Of course He could have. He's omnipotent. Was God with me in all that pain and suffering? Of course He was. He's omnipresent. Was there a reason for all the physical pain and mental anguish I went through? Yes, there was. God is sovereign. He's also very economical. He doesn't waste an experience. In another chapter, I talk more about the miscarriage and why I think it had to happen the way it did.

My husband decided to call his detailer and ask for shore duty. Lester explained the hardship it was on the both of us for him to be gone out to sea with my diabetes and having just experienced a miscarriage. The detailer agreed to give him shore duty in Bremerton, Washington. We left Charleston in June of 1974. Saying goodbye to my then-best friend was very heart-wrenching, but we are still in touch today. I've been thinking about Charleston lately and even wanting to go back and visit, but I realize it was not for a good reason. I had a lot of miserable times in Charleston, and two-thirds of the time, Lester was not there because he was on patrol. So why do I look back and say to myself, *Those were the good ole days*, if I was so miserable? Maybe the answer is that I had my youth, even though I had depression, Tourette's syndrome (undiagnosed), diabetes, and a miscarriage,

Lester took the USS Holland AS34 from South Carolina to Bremerton, Washington, which took a couple of months; and I went back home to Connecticut to wait for the word to fly out to Bremerton, our next duty station. So there I was, back on Aberdeen Street again with the memories of all the "mind garbage" when the irrational fears and anxiety began to come in like a Tsunami, and I felt as though I was back in that same time frame I was in while I lived there in 1970.

Before long, the anxiety, the fear, and finally the depression settled in and covered every single part of my body like a blanket coming down on me, replacing any air that was left with a gravitational, silent sucking. I was back in my same bed in the same bedroom, and I couldn't shake off the bad memories. The smell of my mother's cooking, the smell of the hallway, the New Yorkish accents of people in New England. Everything was taking me back in time. The crazy thing was that except for the fact that it was really 1974, mentally I was back in 1970 and 1971 again.

I stayed in Stamford approximately two months, waiting to leave for Washington State, but at the same time feeling frightened to go that far away from home and start all over. *It would be different*, I thought, if I were normal and able to look forward to my new experience with anticipation and excitement, but that wasn't the case at all. It was just like the trip to California where there had been no joy, no great anticipations about meeting Lester's family, no sense of adventure, just fear, depression, and anxiety and oh yes, the tics. This time, I got so bad that I had to see a doctor. I even asked to be put in the hospital because I couldn't tolerate living.

I could see the toll that my mental illness was taking on my mother as she tried to keep me calm. One night, she went with no sleep while she prayed and stayed with me in the same room. I remember being afraid that she was going to fall apart on me because I had seen the look of weariness written on her face as she suffered through the months worried about me. During this time, she was also the sole caretaker for my grandmother who was suffering from a form of dementia.

September came, and I was getting ready to leave for Seattle where Lester would be waiting for my plane to arrive. I will never forget that it just happened to be Labor Day because I accidently mailed my plane ticket in a mailbox in the airport instead of mailing an insurance policy I'd bought to make my mother the beneficiary should the plane crash. Since it was Labor Day, it was against the law to open any mailboxes. So there I was, with no plane ticket and my plane loading. I scurried around the airport, crying and asking distinctive looking people where I should go and what to do. Nobody knew. Finally, I made a beeline for my gate and, with tears in my eyes, explained the mistake I'd made to the man at the gate. His take on it all? "Lady, this story is so absurd it has to be true. Here, get on the plane." He scribbled something on a fake ticket, and they accepted it. I was on my way to Seattle (with my bottle of Valium) again.

CHAPTER 13

The New State and Friends I Came to Love

A childlike nervousness filled me as I began to slowly digest the fact that I was 3,200 miles away from home in Stamford. As far as I was concerned, I might as well have been on the moon. Yes, I had my Valium, but who would fill it when I ran out? I wasn't at my local friendly pharmacy at home anymore, where nobody asked questions about getting multiple refills. That reality easily motivated me to quickly hook up with a doctor. I decided I was bad enough to see a psychiatrist. Oh boy, did I qualify! I was having panic attacks before they were even called that. I couldn't drive without shaking everywhere, and that didn't include the head ticking which became so bad that I had to actually lie down on my couch and hold my head with my hands to get relief. My psychiatrist put me on an antidepressant. At first, it caused very vivid sleep disturbances in the early morning hours. But eventually it mellowed me out, and I was able to cope.

I have always wanted to play piano, so my husband promised me that when I got to Washington, we would go look at pianos with the idea of purchasing one. We did just that, and soon I was taking piano lessons from a very old lady named Myrtle Siewart. I hated to practice because it made my tics worse, and I couldn't concentrate on the note reading. The complexity of trying to train my hands and read notes at the same time caused me to tic excessively. It was a very complicated and tedious exercise. I was never ready for my next lesson and always dreaded going to it. It was, in ways, like being back in elementary school. If not for wanting so much to learn how to play the piano, I never would have forced myself to continue the lessons.

Sherry, My Concentrated Friend

I recently read a book called *God's Guest List* by Debbie Macomber, a well-known author, especially here in the Northwest where she resides. It's a Christian book about the people that God brings into our lives for one reason or another and how they can become lifetime friends, like my dear friend Lucy, or maybe it's someone who comes along for a short time (but a very rich time) to teach us something or help us. Sherry was definitely one of those people on God's guest list for me. God already knew that coming out to Washington State wasn't going to be so great for me right off the bat, but I'm glad God doesn't let us know how things are going to go and then get our opinion on whether He should do something different according to our plans. He always knows best.

Sherry was a friend even before I moved to Washington State. She helped us get our first apartment and took care of a lot of paperwork and things I probably will never know about because I wasn't there yet. Her husband and mine were on the same ship and came to Washington state together. Sherry could not have helped noticing my head ticking and the nervous state I always seemed to be in, but it didn't seem to bother her at all. She took things in stride. For instance, her green Ford Pinto (remember those?). It refused to shut off even when she would stop the car and take the key out. It would rattle for a few minutes before finally giving up. Her reaction was to just look at me in the passenger seat and smile or laugh and shake her head. But trying to get it to start when you wanted to go somewhere was next to impossible. It did imitate a horse, or better yet, a mule. Sherry was smart as far as I was concerned and not because she had some degree but because she had foresight. She investigated, explored, and considered her options about situations.

I'll tell you about a marvelous plan she had which gave me self-confidence, motivation, self-determination, and challenged me at the same time. She signed us up for a ceramic class on base. It was an eight-week class that covered everything one needed to know to use the ceramic molds and clay, etc. When the eight weeks were up, we took the required test and passed. It was nerve-racking for me, but I did pass.

I remember my head ticking so much in that little ceramic shop that I ached, and it was very embarrassing at times. But it didn't seem to bother Sherry that we were together in the shop and other people there were staring at me. What I'll never forget is how learning all about ceramics and loving to create as I painted changed the course of my thoughts as I anticipated going down to the shop to pick up a finished product to see what it would look like after it had been fired in the kiln. It was in the fall, and I began to make things for family members and friends for Christmas. I was always thinking about the next ceramic project I was going to do. Thanks to Sherry, I spent more time with a brush in my hand or whatever tool I needed, concentrating on how to get the latest project just right.

When I experienced severe panic episodes while living upstairs from Sherry, all I had to do was call her on the phone and tell her of my plight, and she would show up at my door and just hold me and say, "You'll be okay," until I was. She took Lester's place when he couldn't be there to comfort me.

Sherry's stubborn little Pinto provided a refuge for my unending condition, and God also used her radio for similar purposes. Set on a Christian station, it would often play the song, "One Day at a Time, Sweet Jesus," by Christi Lane. I wasn't familiar with the song, but Sherry was. And whenever it played, she would sing along with it with such enthusiasm. That song ministered to me as I listened. I finally learned the song and sang along with Sherry as we drove around in her pinto. I see these times as part of God's providential planning when He called a break in my world of anxiety, depression, and fear.

Sherry's husband and mine were on the same ship and liked to hunt together. When they did, Sherry would invite me for dinner.

It was always elbow macaroni with spaghetti sauce in Tupperware bowls, served with spoons instead of forks, and it was delicious. It wasn't delicious because it was cooked by some great Italian cook. It was delicious because it was comforting to be at her house where I felt wanted and was comforted as I waited with her for our husbands to get back home from their day hunting trips.

Both of our families eventually moved into Navy housing after our numbers came up, and we continued our friendship until they got stationed in Scotland and left us behind in Bremerton.

I call Sherry my "concentrated friend" because although she was in my life for such a short time in comparison to friends I've known so much longer, those two years were packed with so much friendship and good life lessons which I have come to cherish now more than before, so she reminds me of concentrated orange juice (before you add the water).

Friends Who Became Family

Judy and Pat became our new next-door neighbors. Judy was pregnant, with her second child due in December. Pat, like my husband, was also in the Navy, so they never ran out of things to talk about and became very good friends. Judy was fun to be with and still is. Whoever you are, when you're with Judy, you can hang loose in her presence and relax and feel accepted. We are still very close friends to this day, and we've loved and tolerated each other through the last forty-five years.

Loretta, an overly sweet and smiley person, is full of energy and ready to give God the glory for all he has done for her in her life. When we met, she was a brand-new Christian with two small daughters and a Navy husband, and she took every opportunity to show me how God answers prayers. My first "miracle" happened on top of the old JCPenney's parking lot. My car wouldn't start when we got ready to leave, and of course I got mad, not Loretta. She just asked if I wouldn't mind taking her hand in prayer and asking God to help us get the car started. Reluctantly, I did, and to my surprise, before we got finished praying, a man came out of nowhere and up to my car and asked if he can help us. I don't remember what was wrong with the car, but he did something. It started, and we drove home.

While this "mechanical miracle" was taking place, I had mixed feelings of anger but also wonder. I can't even explain why I was angry. I just was. I also couldn't explain exactly why the car started. Of course, my moody ways kept me wondering how I had a friend like Loretta who was not used to being in the company of people who are angry, depressed, and generally in a bad mood all the time. She always gives God the glory for the hurdles in her life whether you want to hear about it or not. This was God working in her, showing the love of Jesus to me whether I wanted it or not. We would turn out to be best friends in the years to come.

Despite my diabetes and the miscarriage and the obvious risk that I would face in becoming pregnant, the desire to have a baby now became very strong in me, but I was told that I would have to quit smoking and get my blood sugar very stable and keep it that way until after I delivered the baby. I already knew it would be a complicated pregnancy, so I gave myself one month to quit smoking. I had the date set for July 11, 1975. I had my last cigarette on that day. That was one of the best decisions I ever made. In fact, I probably wouldn't be alive today had I not quit when I did.

About two months later, I conceived. This time around, I was ready to be pregnant and knew within the first month of conception. I had to be proactive in this journey, and it was some journey, one I will never forget nor regret.

I breathed a sigh of relief once I got through the first trimester because I constantly worried about miscarrying. I was put on a strict diet of 1,500 calories a day and had to stick to it diligently. I had my exchange list of various foods that I could eat with the amounts per serving and my plastic measuring cups for noodles, cereal, rice, and the like.

As I began my second trimester, I started going to the doctor once a week. This was a must because as the pregnancy progressed, I had to keep my blood sugar stable in order to deliver a full-term baby. Of course, I knew that I had a high risk pregnancy at conception and that anything could happen at any time. My hormone levels had to be checked frequently for any signs of inner turmoil. Back in the seventies, checking blood sugar was primitive. You'll recall me telling you that I had to pee in a cup and use a Clinitest pill with ten drops of water and five drops of urine, then place the Clinitest pill in the test tube and watch what color it turns. Then I compared it to a chart to let me know how much sugar was in my blood. If the test indicated that I had high sugar, I would have to go straight to the hospital and get a blood test to determine where my blood sugar was. Most of the time, the blood test revealed that it was about 150 which was acceptable, so I was relieved after one of those visits to the Navy hospital.

It was May of 1976, and I was about five months pregnant when I met yet another lifelong friend who was the wife of a sailor in the Navy working with Lester. Her name was Joanne. She was quiet and reserved and a bit of a health nut when I met her. She had a hardy laugh with strong beliefs, and yes, one of those beliefs was in Christ. Although we were almost the same age, she soon became a motherly figure in my life. When I was with her while pregnant, she made sure that I kept my diabetic regimen, even to the point of figuring out the calorie count of the homemade cookies that she baked. I found her to be very methodical and organized with great insight for the day-to-day issues of life.

God has used all of these special women in my life many times and still does. He is in the business of putting people together who will become family when your own family is geographically too far away to be there to help and to tolerate your not-so-good side. That is God working on our behalf even when we don't know or deserve it.

Judy, Loretta, and Joanne are still in my life; and we are closer than ever before as forty-five years have passed and woven us tightly together through good times and through sorrow. I suppose that my friendship with them will get even sweeter until the end of time on this earth. I believe that God brought Sherry into my life only for a season of time. She had unique gifts which she utilized while befriending me. I treasure the memory of those times though they were some of the roughest I'd been through, but isn't that what bittersweet is all about?

CHAPTER 14

Becoming a Child of the King

Most people know that the Seattle Space Needle is the landmark of Seattle. But there was once a building that stood quite proud and was built as a multipurpose building to hold baseball games, concerts, etc. It was called the Kingdome because it was built in King County in Seattle, and of course, it was shaped like a dome. The capacity of the Kingdome was about 77,000 people at once. Sadly, it was demolished only twenty-five years after building it. How sad to watch the implosion on TV.

It was May of 1976, and I was five months pregnant. An incredibly special speaker was going to be at the Kingdome for three nights. This very special speaker was none other than Reverend Billy Graham. He would be there for three nights. My husband and I were invited to go by our friends Joanne and Sam, and we accepted the invitation to go on May 15.

I already knew that I was going to go forward when the invitation was given to obey God's call on my life and to be forgiven of my sins by accepting the price Jesus paid when He died for me. What an experience it was to see so many others come to Christ as they came forward from the bleachers all the way down to the center of the Kingdome. My husband was one of them. Reverend Graham talked to us and gave us instruction as his staff gave out literature. We prayed and then went home on the ferry. It was extremely late at night, and we walked from the Kingdome to the ferry back to Bremerton just as we came, catching the last ferry going to Bremerton for the evening. There were approximately 77,000 people there on that one night in the Kingdome.

I didn't see stars or have any kind of experience that some people talk about, but without a doubt, I know that I did what I was supposed to do when I went forward with my husband after the call with the choir singing, "Just as I Am."

Having diabetes meant that I had to take my Clinitest kit with me to the crusade and find a bathroom to check my blood sugar with my little urine cup, eyedropper, test tube, and Clinitest tablets. I thought that it was quite a miracle that my blood sugar stayed in the normal range for such an eventful night and all the walking to and from the ferry. God was already helping. He knew and preordained this whole event so I would be able to keep my attention where it needed to be—on what was being said to me by this great man of God.

Almost immediately, I began to have a desire to read the Bible and talk about spiritual things with my husband and my close friends Loretta, Judy, and Joanne and their husbands. Going to church after this experience made me very emotional, especially when we sang songs. The tears would flood my eyes as I sang hymns. I could tell that I was changing on the inside. Soon it seemed like Lester and I could not get enough of God's Word. Sometimes we would get into arguments on a certain verse, but we learned that it was just Satan trying his best to ruin what we had. As time went by, we learned that being a born-again Christian would not be an easy life. In fact, it would even be harder because God's Word says, "The thief cometh not, but for to steal, and to kill, and to destroy. I am come that they may have life and that they might have it more abundantly" (John 10:10, KJV).

The Baby's Coming! Now?

Have you ever been awakened by a very late-night ringing phone about one or two in the morning, and you just know it's going to be bad news? Then it turns out to be a wrong number? After your heart quits beating 200 bpm, you can finally go back to sleep. Then there are those times when the phone rings in the middle of the day, and it turns out to be an emergency—yours. That is what happened to me in July 1976 when my ob-gyn doctor's office called and said that my hormone levels were very dangerous and that I had to get to Madigan Army Hospital in Fort Lewis, Washington, "right now" because it was quite possible that I would give birth to the baby that night. My husband wasn't even home from work yet, but as soon as he walked through the door, we left.

The neonatal ward at the Madigan Army Hospital was one of the finest at that time, and the baby would need all the help it could get to survive. It was about a one and one half hour drive to the hospital during rush hour traffic. We would be driving on Interstate 5 most of the way. My mother always uses the expression "My heart is in my mouth" when she was scared, and that's just where my heart was then.

When we finally arrived and I got admitted, I was sent down to a maternity ward for complicated pregnancies with at least ten other women in a very large hot and humid room with only a pulled curtain for privacy. Some of those expecting were hoping, hopelessly at times, as I would later learn that the best that some of the women could hope for was to carry their babies long enough to deliver with only a faint chance of their offspring surviving. This became my concern as I entered the doors of that hospital and began my two weeks of rigorous tests, along with twenty-four-hour urine collections. (I'll explain that fun run later.) One test consisted of having a B-scan which is known today as an ultrasound. I had one every other day. The hard part was having to fill my bladder with two quarts of water before I had the test. I sometimes had to wait for the pregnant lady ahead of me who was still having her scan, therefore having to hold my two quarts of water in longer than I anticipated. The more water in the bladder, the more accurate the test was. I never knew the sex of the baby because I didn't know that I can ask, so therefore, everything I bought for the nursery was yellow. I didn't go into labor that night, and I'm glad I didn't. Had I gone into labor, it would have not been a miscarriage because I was already seven months. It would have been stillborn or a very sick baby.

Now I know from experience that God's Word is true. Two of my Bibles have become so marked up (especially the Psalms), so I know where to go and what to read for the appropriate need. I found much comfort in the Book of Psalms, and what comfort it is to know that God's Word was not only for the people in the Bible but for you and for me. Also, He is omnipotent, omnipresent, and omniscient; so take Him at His word.

The next morning, I met the doctor who would be the one to make the decisions about my unborn baby, and he definitely wanted me to carry it to full term and to have it there at the Army hospital instead of home in Bremerton where my doctor wanted me to have a C-section. That meant that I would have to stay there until September since my due date, according to this doctor, was September 4. It was only July and the hottest on record. We had no air conditioning, just large fans with open windows.

I didn't realize this, but pregnant women in the heat of summer, waiting for such an important event to happen with complications can sometimes get very bent out of shape. I usually minded my own business and read my Bible or watched TV. I was also reading a book called *Men in Black* by Johnny Cash.

My daily routine at Madigan was to get awakened at 5:30 a.m. and have the baby's heartbeat checked. I remember the *whoosh, whoosh* sound it made as the nurse held the stethoscope to my belly. I loved hearing it because it meant that all was okay with the baby for the time being. Then I would get out of bed and get weighed. I had to be the skinniest pregnant woman there as I only weighed 125 pounds. The reason for that was because I was on an 1,800 calorie diet to keep my blood sugar normal They measured and weighed all that I ate and served it up under one of those mystery lift-up tops. This 1,800 calorie diet was also so the baby won't get too big as diabetic mothers have large babies.

I had to have a certain test taken to let my doctor know how the baby tolerated labor pains. I would be hooked up to a Pitocin drip, and then they would wrap a belt around my belly. And when I would get a contraction, it would record the baby's heartbeat. At one of these tests, my contractions would not stop even after they took the Pitocin drip out. They lasted for two hours, and I was getting very anxious, worried that I would actually go into real labor. The contractions finally did stop, and I ate a well-deserved lunch. Whew!

I did get tempted by the devil himself one day while in the TV room. A lady left her cigarette and told me to watch it until she gets back. It happened to be the very brand I smoked. I believe that it was a true test from God, and I am glad that I passed the test. Praise the Lord. I believe this next event was supposed to happen and may be the sole reason why I was here at Madigan. As you know from reading this far, the chapters are filled with my struggles with Tourette's syndrome, severe anxiety, and OCD which was still tearing at me even though I was now a new person in Christ. I took no medicine during my whole pregnancy. I often wondered how I would take care of my baby.

As I was leaving the ward one day with my pass in my hand, there to my right side, I spotted a room-in mother and baby who had already been born. All I had to do was look at that scene as I walked by, and something happened to me that took those fears away and replaced them with joy and anticipation of becoming a mother. I remember this experience like it was yesterday. It spoke to my heart and spirit so much. I couldn't resist the peaceful feeling that came over me. Oh, I still struggled with the OCD, Tourette's, depression, and anxiety; but I needed to see that new mother and infant. God was waiting for me to go by and look in that room. I went by again and again once I realized they were there. Every time I peeked in, I got that same good feeling. I know now that God was working to prepare me for that same afterbirth joy and comfort.

Can you see how I believe God's timing was perfect for me to be in this place? After all, I didn't know anybody and only got to see my husband for a few hours in the evening, and that was only because they let him off of work two hours early every day so he could drive that I-5 south corridor before rush-hour traffic. Normally I would have been miserable and depressed by these circumstances, but I wasn't. Instead, although I was feeling homesick, I was hopeful and filled with anticipation.

I did have special privileges as I was not sick in bed. I got to roam around most parts of the hospital when I got bored, and I did get bored. I was even able to get a pass to go home for a weekend. The first thing I did was take a hot bath. We weren't able to take baths at the hospital (only showers.) I remember vividly not wanting to go back on Sunday night, but I did, like a good girl. And of course my husband was doing the driving, so I had zero chance of not going back.

Earlier I said I would tell you about the urine (estriol) test that I had to take every other day at the hospital, which consisted of the same routine I did at home. Even though it was a very serious test that gave the doctors priceless information and was what got me there in the first place, the test preparation was very comical. The reason being was that there were several of us expecting women keeping our urine on ice for twenty-four hours. What was so funny was that all of us taking this test carried this very large stainless steel bowl and had to take it with us everywhere we walked and drain the water from the bowl and replace it with fresh ice. We all looked so funny walking around the ward holding our bowls at our hips, just waiting for a "free day" when we didn't have to collect our urine and save it in a bowl for twenty-four hours. It was great being able to pee in a toilet again.

Being so far away from home was one obstacle I had to tolerate, but I didn't do this well. I did want to stay and have the baby full term with this new doctor who wanted the education and the experience. I understood that, but I did finally go back to Bremerton after two weeks were up. Obviously, my estriol levels were fine. I did feel honored that he wanted to take up my case.

They were good weeks. They had to be. God put me there on purpose to see things I needed to see, especially that mother rooming with her baby and, of course, for the technology, which was state of the art then.

CHAPTER 15

For You Are Beautiful

Prior to going in and having my baby, an amniocentesis was performed to ensure that the baby had fully developed lungs, and it did. Today this is a quite common test, but not so in 1976. The date to give birth was set up just like an appointment. I would have the baby on Monday, August 2, even though, according to my naval hospital doctor, I was due on August 12. My ob-gyn doctor in Bremerton believed that the baby was growing too much, too fast; and since diabetic mothers are notorious for this happening, he wanted to get the baby out before it grew too big, as often happens with diabetic mothers in the last months of pregnancy. Ten days would have made a big difference in the size of the baby.

I packed my clothes, and off I went with my husband to have my baby on Monday morning. Needless to say, I was very nervous. I had much more confidence in the doctor at the Madigan Army Hospital who was a lot nicer and had a top-notch bedside manner. However, I had made my decision to come back to Bremerton, so off we went to the naval hospital in Bremerton to have our baby.

All the necessary preparations were made by the nurses, and then I just lay there with a Pitocin drip, experiencing contractions but not even dilating one centimeter. I had no pain to speak of, and I was in a room by myself. I hardly saw my husband, and every once in a while, the doctor would stick his head in and check me for dilation. After eight hours had gone by, he said, "We're going to do a C-section." It was about 3:00 p.m. when they took me up to surgery. I had a spinal block because they didn't want to give me drugs for fear of the baby ingesting them knowing the delicate condition it was most likely in. I was familiar with spinal blocks but nonetheless afraid of having another one, and it was all happening too fast. The Lamaze classes that we took so I could have a natural childbirth turned out to be a waste of time, but that was the least of our worries. I lay there waiting for the spinal medicine to take effect, and Lester was not allowed in the delivery room with me. We were both impressed later after learning that the doctors who were in the delivery room with me were the ones in charge of each department they were representing, including my OB doctor.

After they cut me, it turned out the baby was breech, and they had to turn the baby's body around. That is when the pain started, even though I was totally numb from my chest to my toes. They weren't contractions, but the pain was so bad that I remember yelling for them to stop it. I never closed my eyes once. I talked a lot, asking questions like "what's happening?" and "is the baby all right?"

Finally, at 4:15 p.m., Sandra Marie Stoddard was born. I got only a one-second look at her as they whisked her off because she was definitely in stress from my diabetes. It turned out she was one month premature. Lester was right outside the door and could hardly see her for more than a moment. He was all alone and didn't see me until they brought me back to my private room. We had a name picked out for a girl, and if it was a boy, it would have been Joseph Daniel, the middle names of both her uncles.

Complications were taking place in the nursery right after her birth, but I actually didn't know anything about her condition until the next day. In fact, I didn't see her at all for two days except for the one-second afterbirth. The morning after her birth, I learned from a conversation with a nurse that she had almost stopped breathing but that she was okay. For some reason, I felt total peace. It had to be God's presence surrounding me because I never would have responded by not reacting to such scary news.

Until she could breathe on her own, she had to be on a respirator. I could not get out of bed to see or hold her because I was cut for the C-section. I had to take glucose intravenously because my insulin dependency went down so fast after the baby was born. Sandra also had hyperglycemia, was jaundiced, and had the bilirubin lights on her with her eyes totally covered. (These lights help a baby get rid of the bilirubin that is released into the blood when red blood cells break down.) The worst and most dreadful looking sight was watching her body go into jerky movements from certain imbalances such as calcium and magnesium. They had to immediately shave one side of her head by her temple to put in an IV, and I'm not totally sure what problem was being altered by them doing this. Perhaps the IV was the glucose she needed for the low blood sugar.

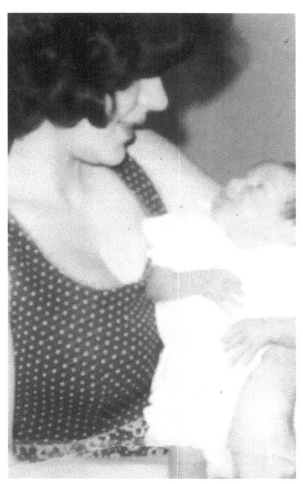

Needless to say, it was heartbreaking to see all the medical equipment attached to her but keeping her stable enough that she did not have to be transferred to another neonatal unit such as Madigan. She weighed five pounds eight ounces at birth but went down to four pounds eleven ounces. They gave me pain medication and waited for it to kick in so I could walk down the hallway, and it was a slow walk as I anticipated all that would take place for the first time I saw and held her. She was in an incubator, of course. I made it to the nursery, and they sat me down so I could finally hold her. That's when she went from their hands to mine, and I held her in my arms for the first time.

My husband was watching from outside through the window, and it was a very tender moment for both of us. I, like many other mothers, will never be able to fully explain the unexplainable. It was like fireworks going off, but on the inside of me. She was so fragile, so tiny, and so sick. I already loved her. All the pain (physical and emotional), the weekly doctor appointments, the hospital stay, and all that blood sugar testing and worrying was so very much worth it. She was alive and going to live!

Nursing her was not an option as she did not have the energy to latch on, and I was just as inexperienced as she was. In those "primitive" days, there were no nurses to teach new mothers how to breastfeed and help them gain confidence and skills before going home. I saw that with my daughter's first child in 2001. How different things are now.

I had to have a shot to dry up my milk, and it broke my heart to know that I would be unable to nurse when I knew that my breast milk was the best for her, even more so in the condition she was in. My pediatrician helped me through this hard process by letting me know that the most important thing was that she got nutrition in her and that I was doing the right thing. She did begin to gain weight. They moved me in a room closer to the nursery, and I began to get visits from her coming to me in a little bundle wrap by the nurses in my new little (and it was little) room.

Do you remember my experience in watching a new mother and child when I was pregnant? As in that mother's room, I also had the yellow curtain that separated me from the next mother. Now I was living that sweet taste of the joy of motherhood. So much had happened, but I was full of joy and peace—the kind of joy that can only come from Jesus—and He was supplying it as each hour and day went by. Oh, by the way, Sandra Marie Stoddard was smallest but most beautiful baby in the hospital. Just ask Daddy.

In an earlier chapter, I talked about the horrible day when I had my miscarriage, saying I believed there was a reason for it and all the pain that I had to experience that day. This is what I believe. I said that God knew the miscarriage was going to happen and that He could have kept it from happening. I also said that God was with me in all the pain and suffering. Those statements are all true.

Another truth that I believe God has planted in my heart is that the labor pains that I suffered so much with the miscarriage in 1974 were part of His plan because He knew ahead that I would want to have the experience of labor pains in childbirth. God surely took care of that with the miscarriage.

Because of the sin of Adam and Eve, God told Eve this, "I will greatly multiply your sorrow and your conception; in pain you shall bring forth children; your desire shall be for your husband, and he shall rule over you" (Genesis 3:16).

So I am glad that I experienced those pains during my miscarriage. I know now what it feels like, and it satisfies me completely. I believe that my first baby is in heaven and that my husband and I will see that child and know it is ours and that he or she will know who we are also, and that brings great joy and anticipation to my heart. Let it also bring joy to your heart if you have experienced a loss of someone whom you know is in heaven as we await that great and glorious day.

CHAPTER 16

The Phone Is Ringing

My daughter was four months old when we finally moved into Navy housing. It was nicer than any place we had lived since moving to Washington state. This meant that we would no longer be neighbors to our three closest friends, the Baileys, the Backuses, and the Conroys; but the fellowship we shared and still share now could not be diminished by a few miles apart. We have grown to love each other like family in the last forty-six years.

My mental state was not okay. I was popping some pills I acquired at the ER one day when I took Sandra in because I thought she wasn't breathing right. Here's what happened. My ticking became so bad while driving to the ER that I had to stop and get help from a stranger by knocking at their door and asking to use the phone to call Pat and Judy. Once we got to the hospital, they checked out the baby, and she was okay. But they could see that I was ticking badly and filled with anxiety. They sent me home with a bottle of Dalmane pills. I took them as long as the pharmacist would fill them, and that was quite a long time. They were really for sleeping, but they kept my ticking at bay so I continued to use them. When I tried to go cold turkey, I couldn't. I was once again addicted. After going for almost one week without a pill, I could not hold my head still for a second, nor could I drive the car in the shape I was in. My husband was not even aware of all of this, and I don't know why he never questioned my obvious behavior. Perhaps because he is a much-focused person who is always preoccupied with something (as you'll understand when you read the next chapter).

The phone rang, and my husband took the call. After a very long and troubling conversation with his brother-in-law, Lester got off the phone and announced that his nephew needed a home to live in permanently because his sister had lost custody of all three of her children because of illness. The plan was for us to take in the youngest child, who was seven years old. After about a week, Matthew Kelly Ryckman was our new family member. He wanted to be called Mark, so that's what we called him. Eventually he became comfortable with calling us mom and dad, but I wasn't at all comfortable with it. In plain English, I was scared.

When we decided to bring him into our home, I still had every problem I started out with in this book. The truth was that I was not ready to mother a seven-year-old little boy whom I knew little about. *How can I not want this child?* I thought. I'm selfish, but more than that, I was just plain scared and skeptical about taking this leap into darkness. I felt that our finances were not able to handle what it would cost to feed and clothe another child. I already had my hands full with a seven-month-old infant. I was a Christian, but I was not relying on God at all. I wondered why I had no peace about this decision. My husband didn't seem to have all these negative attitudes. If he did, he didn't share them. Lester always takes things in stride. This was no different. But this was a human being.

He literally walked into our lives in March of 1977. He was very cute, with shiny reddish brown hair and hazel blue eyes and very talkative but hard to understand. He was a small child. He also was asthmatic, probably had ADD/ADHD. He chewed on things and couldn't sit still or concentrate on anything very long. At times, I was pulling my hair out, trying to understand this child. Obviously, there was going to have to be a major adjustment period for all of us. Trust had to be established between each family member, which was not an overnight process. In fact, I was afraid it would take forever as time went by, and it seemed to be an ongoing process. This boy who had just been torn from his mother's arms to live with almost total strangers and my adjustment to a new baby just seven months old, plus Mark's adjustment to all of us, was a very scary experience.

At the time of Mark's arrival, I felt that he got a bad deal, leaving a bad situation at his home and entering into an even worse one with me having so many complicated issues to deal with, especially ticking. I wondered what he thought of my ticking, which by now was totally out of control from the anxiety of all the newness and adjustment of two children. The dependency of Dalmane was making my ticking worse to where I could not stop ticking at times.

The years passed, and Mark saw fit to have his name legally changed to Stoddard, which made us very proud. He served on the historic battleship, the USS Missouri, during the Persian Gulf War. But the eleven years in between coming and leaving were hard. Looking at things in retrospect will always set one up for feelings of failure, remorse, and disappointment if we let it; and I did many times as a parent.

My son loves us very much, and we love him. My relationship with Mark, although rocky for many years, has had metamorphic results in that we are now two different people with grown-up attitudes because of, and in spite of, each other's differences. The benefits I reap today from his love for me far outweigh the in-between eleven years of touch and go. I know now that I didn't give myself enough credit for the situation I was put into and that I was physically and emotionally stressed prior to Mark joining our family.

After taking early childhood classes at the local community college, I know, without a doubt, that there were some things I could have never changed in Mark because of the disadvantage of my not having him earlier in his life when he was a baby.

Mark and I have developed (or maybe always have had) the same sense of humor. We know how to make each other laugh and exactly what kind of cards to pick out for each other on special occasions. We also love the same kind of comical movies. He also knows how to make me cry; but now they are typically happy tears.

We shared our Christian faith with Mark just as we did our daughter, and we took them both to church and Sunday school. Both were heavily involved in church functions. But my husband

and I learned a golden lesson from this, and that is that we did not spend quality time with each of our children on a one-on-one basis as daughter to father and mother to son and vice versa.

Being involved in church functions can be great, and God wants us to serve in our local church, but being too busy with church functions, whether it's the children's ministry or being a deacon, can put undue stress on the children God has given us to raise. Church ministries should not overinvolve parents to a point where they are neglecting their own duties as the example setters for the very children God has given them. Stressed-out, overcommitted parents should recognize when this is happening and put a stop to it before it infiltrates negativity into the home and the children become victims of overcommitment on the parents' part. My husband and I wish we would have said no more often.

We thank God that our children are Christians, but we do not take the credit because God knows they could have easily gone down a different road. That makes me a very thankful but neurotic mother.

CHAPTER 17

Milking It for All It's Worth: An Ordained Ordeal

Before reading this chapter, one must stretch the muscles of the imagination a bit. It seems that is what my husband Lester did when, at age twenty-seven, he went out and purchased a 1946 Divco milk truck for $500 and drove it home and parked it with the intention of ripping the guts out of it and creating a "home" for Sandra, Mark, and myself. And then he planned to drive all the way to Connecticut (3,200 miles away) with our 1965 Mustang in tow. One must also have a large sense of humor and a belief that "all things work out for the good to those who love the Lord and are called according to His purpose" (Romans 8:28).

This is a story about the human will and endurance, about discouragement, fear, anger, and patience, even danger. It's about a round-the-clock adventure and a story about God's intervention, direction, and protection in the midst of inconceivable circumstances.

Lester and I had been Christians now for about fifteen months, and we were growing slowly but surely. We knew that the only way we could afford to make a trip to Connecticut to see my family and let them meet my children was to drive out there without spending any money on motels or restaurants. Impossible? Of course not! Remember, I'm married to Mr. Adventure, who proposes marriage on the second date, takes me away for one month across the United

States, and purchases a car off a lot and takes me up the Pacific Coast, then down, and marries me in Vegas. You read it all in an earlier chapter. Lester simply cannot turn down a challenge.

The next thing I recall is seeing him pulling into our driveway with this vehicle. It was the ugliest thing I'd ever seen. I hoped he didn't think that we were driving that thing across country. The milk truck sported clown colors of red and yellow, and Lester was fascinated with it as he pondered on its potentiality. Can you see where this is going?

He took me out to meet his milk truck and get a tour of the inside. He described in detail what he had planned on doing to it to make it road-ready. "This baby will look like a regular motor home when I get finished with it," he said. "You see, back here, I plan on building an eating area with two tables and two benches, which will convert into a bed at night. All I have to do is move a few boards and throw down a cushion, and it's a bed for us. Over here will be a space for Sandra's playpen. I'll bolt it to the floor, so it won't move when I stop and go. It will also be her bed. For Mark, I'll build a hammock and connect it to each end of the truck. He'll be able to sleep under the stars with these gigantic windows to look out of."

I couldn't believe my eyes or ears. *This man has lost his marbles,* I thought. Then he continued, "I'll add a gas stove, a sink, a frig, a toilet, air-conditioning, overhead lights [to read in the evening before

retiring], speakers, a CB Radio, wall-to-wall carpeting, and even curtains on the windows for privacy. So what do you think?" he asked.

"I think you're crazy," I said. "And I'll never see my family if
I have to wait for you to do all this." I thought that by the time he
bought all the stuff, he would need to make this a reality, that we
could all fly first class to Connecticut and back.

But he paid no attention to what I thought. It was then six
months before July 1977, which is when we planned to leave, so he
had about that much time to get his act together before this milk
truck was road ready. First, he gutted out the whole insides. I don't
remember where all the insides went and don't care to remember.
The nights got pretty lonely while he worked until dark with just
stopping for supper, then going back and working till bedtime.

The days turned into weeks, then months, and it looked like
maybe there was some small chance that he could pull this off. I
began to see the light at the end of the tunnel as I peeked inside from
time to time to see his progress and began to get excited at the thought
of this crazy plan actually coming to reality. The outside of the truck

itself was an eyesore, but he
said he would prime and
paint it before we left. His
plan was to tow our 1965
Mustang so we could use it
when we reached our destination. He masked the whole
truck and then spray-painted it with a primer red color. It had that
unfinished look, but it remained that way because we were out of
time. He had finished everything he said he would do to the inside,
and I admit I was very impressed. To me, it looked like a rookie/
professional job and that was good enough for me because we were
about to leave for the trip. We may have looked like the Beverly
Hillbillies on the outside, but it's what's on the inside that counts.
And the inside was equal to the comforts of the Beverly Hilton.

Just before leaving, we got a phone call telling us that Lester's
dad had a stroke and was in the hospital. We decided to stop and
see Dad on our way to Connecticut, so we headed first to Portland,

Oregon. As we were leaving for our adventure, I asked Lester if he had ever taken the milk truck for a test drive. He said the only test drive was driving it back from Bremerton, where he'd bought it. I cannot tell you how much I didn't like his answer. Was this part of his adventurous spirit? I didn't know. I had other names for it but didn't express them at the time. I began to get a kind of knot in my stomach with this new information.

We had just reached Chehalis, Washington, when the truck hit a very large bump that instantly knocked out the air conditioning and the water pump. We were stranded. Lester began a very long walk to the nearest car-parts store to try to find a water pump that would work in a 1946 Divco milk truck. Yes, the odds were against us. In the meantime, there was a heat wave going on; and to keep us from cooking, I wheeled Sandra in her umbrella stroller with Mark alongside me in the shade of the truck. My spirit was taking a large tumble as I began to wonder if this was God's will, or were we crazy for even trying this.

Well, my spirit was revived when I saw Lester finally walking back after two hours with a water pump in his hands that would actually fit on this milk truck. The parts store owner was just as shocked as we were as he was very doubtful he'd find anything resembling it. In no time, we were rolling again, but without air conditioning. By the time we reached Portland, we were so tired and dirty and discouraged that we discussed turning back. Here, we met a friend of Dad's, a very elderly Christian lady that had been taking care of some of Dad's needs before he had the stroke. She offered to watch the kids while we went and visited him in the hospital. After we got back to Dad's apartment, we cleaned up the kids and ourselves and settled in at Dad's house for the night, thinking we would decide on whether we should continue with the trip when morning came.

The Christian lady talked to me and said that she would pray about it and call us in the morning. She did just that but with strong advice to go on with the trip and not to turn back after she had talked to the Lord about it. We took her advice and, with renewed strength, went on with our original plans.

Sandra had an ear infection and was on antibiotics, and Mark was carsick and on Dramamine. It was beginning to dawn on us that this trip was going to take more than the four days we had planned. The top speed this blessed vehicle would go was 45 mph. It had no power steering, no power brakes, no power anything. We were all hot, tired, and dirty, and sick of eating cups of noodles. Mark began to lose weight as he couldn't keep anything down because of the excessive heat in the truck. He was even throwing up the Dramamine. The sun was baking us alive in the heat wave that was then sweeping the Midwest. (I have baked cookies in colder ovens.) Sandra seemed to be the only one not suffering much. She seemed happy to just sit or stand in her makeshift play area with her cloth diapers on. Perhaps she knew something we didn't know.

The concept forever was taking on a new meaning. We were rapidly running out of money because of Lester having to fill up so often. I often wondered what we looked like to other vacationers that were passing us on the road in their recreational vehicles. You could see the look in their eyes as they passed us in their Winnebagos with color TV, swivel chairs, and air conditioning, which, you'll recall, we'd lost way back in Washington State. Some of the vacationing kids' faces reflected such thoughts as, *What is that*, *Oh, those poor people*, and *Hey, dad, are those leftover hippies from the sixties?* It was embarrassing at times, and we probably were feeling leftover, just not from the sixties.

I don't recall what state we were in, but we were on a long stretch of road when suddenly a semi passed us on the left and then got back in our lane before clearing us, and Lester had to slam on the brakes to keep us from going off the road into a ditch. Right after the incident, he stopped, and we all caught our breaths and thanked God in prayer for watching over us. I remember sitting on the steps of the milk truck and shaking like Jell-O for a while. Before I even stopped shaking from the semitruck incident, I began to wonder what the next adventure was going to be. Thanks to God, we got to call it an incident, not an accident.

We had reached Nebraska by now. We had been traveling about four or five days. If all had gone as planned, we should have been home or close to it. I had developed a very large boil under my armpit (a very typical thing for me when my blood sugar is out of control), and Mark was so white it looked like somebody had bleached him.

The CB radio shorted out, and that meant it had drained the auxiliary battery that was giving us electricity in the milk truck so we could see and use the stereo. When I couldn't see to change Sandra's diapers, Lester went outside under the hood to try to remedy the situation by connecting one of the lights to the main battery. While he was doing this, he heard a humming static sound and looked up and saw a ball of static electricity on the end of CB antenna. Not good! He did get one light hooked up, but only with God's protection. I know there were angels out there that night. (By this time, I was starting to think we had a whole slew of them.) We went on, with and by God's grace and protection and His appointed angels.

As nighttime approached, we could see that there was a huge electric storm brewing in the skies of Omaha, Nebraska. The heat wave had followed us since leaving on our trip, and it was so hot and humid. The thunder and lightning surrounded us as we drove. I began to pick up a scent of burning rubber. When I asked Lester about it, he gave me the "don't worry, pretty little wife" answer, saying it was just engine oil burning. I didn't buy it. The smell got so bad that even he was becoming suspicious. I immediately yelled for him to stop driving and let me out with the kids. Instead, he jumped out himself, took one look at the brakes, and saw that they were glowing red. When I got out with the kids, we realized that we were stranded in a huge and dangerous storm that was displaying three different sets of lightning in the skies with rain and some of the loudest thunder I'd ever heard. We were standing there outside the milk truck, not knowing where to go, when we saw a man at a gas station who told us that there was a motel about two miles away. The doubts and fears of what would become of us were starting to pour over us as hard as the rain from the skies.

We left everything except what we absolutely needed and walked with the kids, Sandra being wheeled in her umbrella stroller. I had reached my lowest point right then and there, even before starting to walk to the motel. We did get to the motel safely, and I gave the kids much-deserved hot baths and put them to sleep. The portable crib that the motel gave us for Sandra fell through in the middle of the night and down she went with it onto the floor, but she was not hurt. What took place at the motel that night was a testimony of God's guidance and supernatural power as He led my husband back to the broken truck and miraculously gave him the physical power he needed to repair it alone, in that dark and stormy night, as lightning filled the skies.

The kids were asleep when we both knelt down and prayed. We knew we needed God's help in a big way. Lester asked God to baptize him in the Holy Spirit (something he was seeking in his personal Christian life). He then went back out in the storm where the truck was sitting. When he got there, he found that one of the brake drums had cammed over and needed to be taken out and replaced.

This was more than a job for just one person, one that required maximum strength to do what had to be done to get us back on the road again. The brake drum had to come off so that he could get the cammed-over brake released. There was a large nut holding the brake drum on, and he tried using a combination of the tools he had to loosen the nut, but with no success. Then he prayed, "Lord, I can't do this. I need some help." He said that the Lord told him to "take an extension, put it on the corner of the nut, and hit it with a hammer." When he did that, the nut came loose, and he was able to take the drum off. This released the brakes so he was able to adjust them. He drove the truck back to the motel, and it was morning by then. We were back on the road again, as if nothing had ever happened. That night, Lester had asked God for His power and His help, and he received both. John 14:14 says, "If you ask anything in My name, I will do it." As we drove on the next morning, I could see a new and refreshed look on Lester's face, and he seemed so much more cheerful, as though he'd gotten a new lease on life. He actually did.

We were running out of money by now, and by the time we got to Indiana, we were broke. We called home to my brother for enough money to get us to Connecticut, but we had to wait at a truck stand where the Western Union place was. When we went to go get the money the next morning, we learned that it had been sitting there all night. At least we all got some sleep, and we made it to Pennsylvania without much trouble. The heat wave was still in existence; in fact, it stayed throughout the trip. At this point, we'd been on the road for seven days, and many things could have happened even worse than they did. We were grateful to God for our lives. But God was about to remind us that He had been with us through this whole experience, and He was about to remind us once again.

We all heard an awful *bang* but didn't know where it had come from. We turned onto an off-ramp and heard it again. That's when Mark looked out the window and said that the Mustang was driving all by itself. Oh, how we wished he was fooling! Lester finally came to a stop, and we got hit again as the car, which had followed us down the off-ramp, banged into the milk truck. It was Sunday, and we were in need of a bigger ball for the hitch that had come loose. After a few hours of literally driving around in circles, we found a hardware store, got what we needed, and got out of Pennsylvania.

We were driving on the Jersey Turnpike when we noticed police doing a vehicle check. Eventually, they reached us and stepped into the milk truck and asked us if the kids in the vehicle were our children. Apparently, there had been a kidnapping, and they were stopping suspicious-looking vehicles. Suspicious? US? Nine days later, we were on the home stretch; and we were tired, dirty, and hungry for a home-cooked meal. The kids did so great for such a gruesome and even dangerous trip at times. Mark was a trooper.

The Exit Six sign never looked so good to me. We had finally reached our destination. I am ever grateful to God for His provisions, never too early, never too late, and always in the nick of time. We had to sell our 1965 Mustang for just $200 because we couldn't go back home the same way we'd come. The milk truck had all it could take, and we had run out of vacation time because of the unexpected misfortune that seemed to plague us from the beginning of the trip. We packed all of our clothes, Sandra's playpen, and the car seat, and had them shipped home.

We left the milk truck with my brother to eventually sell and mail us a check for whatever he could get for it. With the financial help of my wonderful family, we flew home. I was very sad to say goodbye and leave because I didn't know when we would ever be able to afford to come back again. But I did know this: I wasn't returning in a milk truck.

My husband was, without a doubt, a tower of strength through all of our trials, never once showing signs of weakness, either mentally or physically, but I knew this trip experience had taken a toll on his ego and self-esteem. He was often frustrated with all the unexpected twists and turns and must have experienced much disappointment at times. But at the same time, I watched him grow spiritually, having seen all that God had done for us in those nine days on the road. We often reminisce about the trip and have told many people about it. We laugh now at all the things that took place, but not without the knowledge that God was always in our midst.

We had been home for about a month when I got a phone call from my sister Pinky. After the usual greeting, she said to me, "I did it!"

To which I said, "You did what?"

"I made the decision," she said. She had watched a Billy Graham Crusade on TV and followed through by acknowledging Christ as her Lord and Savior. She called me in obedience to what Billy Graham had said to do, which was to tell someone.

While still in Connecticut, she seemed incredibly open to hearing how our lives had changed since we'd become Christians, and she was impressed by God's provisions for us while traveling 3,200 miles in the milk truck. If anything, this touch-and-go trip started making a difference in the way she had thought about Christianity before.

After her conversion, she began to disciple new Christians and open up her heart and home to many in need. I know that my mother was praying through this whole ordeal because she would talk to me on the phone as we moved from state to state, always assuring me that she was praying us home. Never, never underestimate what a praying mother can accomplish when she gets together with her God. It is awesome how God works. Who can second-guess what He will do and how He will do it and how long He will take?

What A Nut

My brother found a buyer for the milk truck. (He can sell anything.) He let the buyer know that the brakes needed work. We received a phone call from him, asking Lester if the nut that they were trying to loosen was the same nut that he'd had trouble with in Omaha, Nebraska. It seemed they needed to send a mobile unit out to work to see if they could loosen the nut that day. The mobile unit had air-impact tools, but even those could not loosen the nut. Yes, it was the same nut that Lester had struggled with in Nebraska, so they had to tow the milk truck back to a brake shop that had bigger air-impact tools. My brother was very impressed when Lester told him over the phone that the nut was one and the same. They eventually got the nut loose.

The buyer paid $500 for the milk truck, which was exactly what Lester paid for it in the first place. After my brother mailed us the much-needed money, we went out and bought a secondhand car. I often wonder what would have happened (or not happened) had the Christian lady who was taking care of Dad, a perfect stranger, had not cared enough to pray about our unfortunate circumstances. This lady, whom I am sure I will see in heaven someday, was an ambassador of God for a troubled family, one that God used in such an extraordinary way to head us in the right direction for His glory.

CHAPTER 18

Brainstorm: When it Rains, He Pours

The beginning of 1978 was a major year for change in our family. We moved out of Navy housing because Lester's time was up after having served a total of eight years. We bought an old fixer-upper house in Bremerton. Just a month after moving, my father-in-law came to live with us so we could take care of him. Soon after, Lester was hired by Lockheed Missile and Space Co. in Bangor, Washington, now known as Lockheed Martin. Our faith in God had been strengthened during the trip with the milk truck, and we were still attending the same Assembly of God church that we'd been going to when our daughter was born. One would think that I might shy away from Assembly of God churches because of my unpleasant experience in earlier years, but I had gotten over it. And this is where our good friends, Loretta and Steve, Pat and Judy, and Joanne and Sam were worshipping; so it seemed natural, and we were very fond of our pastors.

I don't know what the congregation thought of me as I sat in the pew ticking away uncontrollably, along with sweating from the tension it brought on. I felt the whole congregation was watching, whether they were or not. This went on every Sunday morning, and I thought this was the worst place and time a person would want to be uncontrollably ticking their head and making facial grimaces since somebody might think I had a demon or, even worse, was demon-possessed. Of course, no one knew that I was harboring these thoughts in my head—not even my husband. It was too scary to talk about to anybody.

In spite of all that was going on in my head (worrying about the presence of demons in and around me) and outside of my head with the uncontrollable jerking movements, my husband and I felt it was time that we were baptized in water. This follows a person's conversion to Christianity as a symbol of dying to sin and rising with Christ. This would be a full emersion in the baptismal tank. We filled out all the necessary paperwork while assuring the pastor that we indeed were born-again Christians and wanted to do this as a symbol of our new life in Christ. We followed through and were baptized. "Go therefore and make disciples of all nations baptizing them in the name of the Father and the Son and the Holy Spirit" (Matthew 28:19).

These were times of great inner turmoil for me. Satan did have a field day with my mind as unwanted thoughts and fears flooded me, and I started having anxiety attacks daily. I would allow myself to think of heart-wrenching instances that involved my then-baby daughter, which I would never even think of taking place in my worst dreams, and then I'd imagine that I let the particular thing happen to her. Then inside of me, I allowed myself to feel the heartbreak and suffering it would have caused (as if it really had happened). I could not stop ticking at times, and it would come on in the stillness of the night when all was quiet and everyone else was asleep. Silence was definitely my enemy. I was plagued with a fear that pictures were going to start falling off the walls any second. These bouts with the intrusive, unwanted thoughts would wax and wane through the years, and I still suffer with them now and then. But that is part of the illness, and the medication helps.

My Disorder Finally Gets a Name

It was 1979, and we were all sitting in church as a family. I didn't know that I was being noticed by a particular person. I was

107

about twenty-seven then and, as usual, still ticking and making awful facial grimaces. When the service was over, a lady approached me and began to ask me about my ticking. This woman was no stranger to me. She had even been at my shower when my daughter was born in 1976. I told her I had been ticking since I was a child and that I didn't know why. She wondered if I had ever seen a doctor for it, and I told her of the tests that were taken when I was a child—blood work, brain wave, and neck x-rays. She then gave me the name of a neurologist and advised me to go see him because she said it looked to her like I might have something called Tourette's syndrome. I had never heard of it, but she said she had an adopted son that was diagnosed with it by this particular doctor.

I followed her advice, but not right away. I kept worrying that I wouldn't have this disorder and would therefore go back to square one. I put it off for months before I finally gave in and went and then learned that I did have Tourette's syndrome! So now I had a name for something that had plagued me most of my life. This neurologist gave me Haldol or haloperidol (the drug of choice then) to take for the tics. He told me I could find my own dose by the way that I was feeling. Haloperidol is used to treat psychotic disorders (conditions that cause difficulty telling the difference between things or ideas that are real and those that are not). Haloperidol is also used to control motor tics (the uncontrollable need to repeat certain body movements) and verbal tics.

This drug was not one to play games with, however. I did find some relief from the tics but soon was ticking even worse than I had ever done before. My almost-four-year-old daughter was noticing it and asking me why I was making weird sounds and shaking my head. My head was bonging all over the place, and I couldn't stop the vocalalia and echolalia (the urge to speak out words with no sense or copy what someone else says). *How did one address that problem?* I wondered. I continued trying to regulate my dose by myself until one night, when I couldn't seem to get enough control of the tics.

Then I did something I'd never done before. I began to wake myself up while trying to sleep, and this went on until the wee hours in the morning. Needless to say, I had developed a new phobia; and to this day, I'm not sure if I was being influenced by the Haldol. But that was in 1980, and ever since then, I've suffered bouts with sleeplessness simply because of being afraid that I would wake myself up, therefore fulfilling my own prophecy.

This phobia seemed to replace the fear of hearing voices. I couldn't tell you which one was worse. I just knew that I didn't have the resources to fight it. I had to go on antidepressants and wait for them to kick in to get my life back. Even then, I was not totally cured of the phobia that I would possibly never sleep again. I simply could not shake this fear.

There were times when I couldn't take care of my kids, cook, drive the car, eat, talk on the phone, or care about my diabetes. But then there were times when I felt totally normal without any fear of not sleeping, as if it only existed in my past and I carried out activities like any other normal person by being employed, working out, walking, teaching Sunday school, and being involved in my daughter's elementary school activities, such as being a room mother and teacher's aide. Then there were also times when I found the strength to do all this and still have my phobias and depression.

During these times in my life, so many people came to my aid and ministered to me either by prayer, taking my kids for a day, sharing Scripture with me, or sitting with me for a day when my husband had to work. Food was brought to my house by church members, so I didn't have to cook while in some of my worst "brainstorms." But I can truly say that since 1980, I have had more good days, months, and years than bad ones by a long shot. That is why I titled this chapter "When It Rains, He Pours"—He, of course, being the God of all sorrow and trials as He allowed His Son to go through all the mental, physical, and psychological trauma of knowing He had to die on the cross for our sins and carry the weight of the sins of the world. Christ suffered anxiety and physical pain like no one else ever did, and He was tempted by Satan himself like no one else ever was. Romans 5:5 says, "Now hope does not disappoint, because the love of God has been poured out in our hearts by the Holy Spirit who was given to us."

The Holy Spirit is our comforter in pain. As Christians, we can always rely on the Holy Spirit to comfort us in a way we may not be expecting, as when I heard the guitar playing and how comforting it was for me to sit down with Aunt Lucy and look at photo albums. Both times I felt a feeling of calmness go through my body, just as I did when I saw the lady with her newborn child when I was seven months pregnant. That experience also gave me both peace and feelings of anticipation about having my own child as the Holy Spirit poured on such a sweet peace and a love for my unborn baby. What timing!

One time, when I was in a real pickle (or should I say in the pickle jar) and just filled with fear, depression, and anxiety, I somehow found this verse that got me through the day and was such a comfort, "Unless the Lord had been my help, my soul would have settled in silence. If I say, 'My foot slips,' your mercy, O Lord, will hold me up. In the multitude of my anxieties within me, your comforts delight my soul" (Psalm 94:17–19).

Yes, He is always on time when He pours, and I am reminded that I did not know that any of these times He poured were times that He was ministering to me. You may not know of times like these unless you look back and try to remember them. If I hadn't written this book, I might never have discovered the times He has gotten me out of the pickle jar. Bless God for the gift of the Holy Spirit speaking to us through the Word of God!

CHAPTER 19

Whose Spirit Is It Anyway?

I don't know about you but our family is not perfect—far from it actually. Yes, my husband, children, and I are all Christians; but you might wonder, especially on Sunday mornings. Why is it that things seem to erupt out of proportion on Sunday mornings when we are supposed to be getting ready to sit in God's house and bless His name? I've often found myself fighting mad at my husband or one of my kids as we were entering the door of the church. It would be over a nothing thing, but it was always big enough to set me off.

A good example would be our famous pancake-flipping fight. Lester loves to cook breakfast, and it usually includes pancakes. If one happens to be burning before he gets a chance to flip it, I immediately go into action and grab the spatula and flip it so it won't burn. This sets him off like a rocket blasting into space. So our argument would be about how I offered my help, but he did not want any help; he had it all under control. This would set me off, and I'd carry that anger right to church with me and then put on my pretend happy face when I entered the church.

Perhaps because of my Tourette's syndrome, mixed with the diabetes and depression, I tend to be very edgy and can't seem to let things like this just ride instead of having to argue everything out. Maybe it would be that way if I were "normal." Either way, my husband and I have often sought counseling for marital difficulties, mainly communication problems.

One time in particular, we sought counseling from the pastor of the church we were attending. We, of course, were attending an Assembly of God church because our beliefs were strong about their doctrine. In this particular counseling session, I was upset about Lester's overcommitments with church programs, mainly involving boys ministry and all the time and involvement that went with it. This pastor knew of my ticking and knew that I had something, but I don't know if he knew what it was.

We had joined this church in 1980 or 1981. By the time we came in for our first counseling session, he knew me very well; in fact, I was prayed for in this church many times, and a few times there was even a "word of knowledge" about someone who had a "problem in their neck" and needed to go up for prayer. The whole church knew of me and my tics, and I felt obligated but scared to go up for prayer while people laid hands on me and prayed for my "neck problem." This always proved to be embarrassing for a few reasons. One was that I never did get healed, and I wondered what the congregation thought of my faith in God. The other was because I thought my face looked ugly when I was ticking, and I felt that people wished I would just quit worshipping there and attend another church.

I was also afraid that people in the congregation thought I might have a demon, or worse, be demon-possessed. As I explained earlier, these fears were derived by my own thoughts; but at the same time, something spoken on the subject of demons or demonic powers in the congregation helped foster these thoughts into being realistic in my head.

I was team teaching first and second grade Sunday school at this time, and when I look back now, I don't quite understand why the pastor allowed me to teach Sunday school and do other things as a leader of children. It's what he said to me in the counseling session that made me wonder why he would approve of me being in any ministry position at all.

The pastor was speaking to me and my husband in the counseling session regarding my husband's busyness in the church. Then he suddenly pointed out just how awful it looks when I tic, and he said something like this, "People can get all kinds of ideas from looking at you, you know." This criticism was totally out of context for the reason we were there, and he had already taken my husband's side in the debate about him being gone so much and me having the two kids and my father-in-law to take care of, which was more than I could handle with all I had to deal with. The session ended quickly as he had a pressing date to fulfill, and I left so upset that I literally didn't want to go back to the church again or even go home with my husband.

All I wanted was the truth about our situation with some understanding and a Christian response as to whether my husband was fulfilling his duties as a Christian husband or if he was putting church responsibilities first. Was I a big whiner? We never finished the session, and it was the last one we went to with that pastor. I did have great respect for his preaching, however, and was thoroughly fed by it for that particular season in my life. I still see him once in a blue moon at weddings and funerals.

I laid aside my hurt and anger, and we went to church the next Sunday as if nothing had been said. I still taught Sunday school and occasionally volunteered for the girls ministry if they needed someone for an overnighter or a Wednesday night substitute.

The truth is, if anybody ever could have gotten into my mind in those days from the early 1980s on, they would have really believed that I did have some form of demonic oppression, at least. But the true friends I had in that church who really knew me back in those days knew that I was a true born-again Christian, and they treated me like a sister in the Lord, for which I remain grateful. I always felt the love from my brothers and sisters in the Lord at this church, regardless of my head jerking and facial grimaces. But there was still that lurking feeling when, on a Sunday morning in an Assembly of God "Spirit-filled" church, I'd see someone staring at me and would have loved to give them a penny for their thoughts. Some I didn't have to give that penny to.

Soon, they would be approaching me with some information that God "told them to tell me." I, being very intimidated, gullible, naive, and unsure of myself would think that anything they had to say to me had to be from God because they were bigger and better, prettier, more spiritual, or smarter than I was and should be heard. This type of thing only went on at Pentecostal gatherings. I began to believe that these people who approached me from time to time had a little of their own spirit involved in ministry, perhaps more than the Holy Spirit's involvement. And I was absolutely right for the most part. Here is another example.

While attending this same church, I noticed a new face in the congregation but thought nothing of it until that face kept looking back at me from where he was sitting. A few Sundays later, I found that he was sitting next to me, which was far from the spot he usually sat in (which was on the other side of the church in a congregation of about four hundred people). He got my attention and then asked me if I would go with him after the service because he wanted to "help" me. Lester was on the other side of me and didn't know that he had asked me to go with him. I was so shaken by this that I couldn't wait until the service was over to see what was going to transpire with this man's strange request.

I think that he probably thought he could pray my tics away. Perhaps he wanted me to meet some other people who would perform an exorcism on me. I was frightened. As the service drew closer to an end, I could feel my body start to heat up, and I begin to sweat and tic excessively. Finally, when the service was over, I told Lester what this man requested; and he would not agree to go or let me go with him by myself, of course. I told the man no, and that was the end of that episode.

I knew the out-of-character thoughts I was thinking and how weird my life had gone up until now, but other people couldn't get into my brain. And I know that now, but it took a long time for me to be convinced that the Spirit of the living God had come into my life the moment I received Jesus in 1976 at the Seattle Kingdome while five months pregnant. And He was with me before my conversion because He knew that I would surrender my life to Him because He knows everything. Who else could it have been that comforted me in those younger years as a child when I was the elephant in the room?

Yes, Satan did and still does have a heyday with my mind, especially when I allow myself to go back to those days of naivety, allowing people to minister to me by the way of overkill. I've learned that it's not running all over the place trying to get someone to pray demons out of me that is imperative. It's opening my Bible, singing to the Lord, praying and meditating on His Word, and being silent. That is what brings peace and rest. Yes, I'm on medication, but that is also a provision from the Lord, just as pumping insulin is for me to be able to stay alive.

Yes, our family did remain unstable and malfunctioned; and I did have depression, anger, and fear to such a degree that I thought I'd die, but I didn't. Yes, I ran my husband around to every husband-wife seminar that I could get him to come to. Did it help? No. I obviously had the same problem of letting my own spirit take control and forgetting all about the Holy Spirit moving when He chose to do so, not when I wanted Him to. Did my husband stop all of his ministries in the church after a knockdown, drag-out fight with him? No, he didn't.

When we finally left the AG church and went to another denomination, my husband did give up a lot of church ministry, and we started anew with another church where we remained for ten years and where he served only as a deacon. It was during these years that both of us realized that we had not spent as much time with our own children as we'd spent with other people's children. We both regret that now. We have both been forgiven by God for our neglectfulness to our children and to each other.

I truly believe that everybody who has ministered to me for anything in my past has done it in good faith and with the intention of helping me. And sometimes it was helpful, and God did touch me. I just think that some people are overzealous while not under the calling of the Holy Spirit before they approach me. As you have read in this chapter, I have made my own mistakes, doing the same thing when I convinced my husband that we needed this or that seminar for our marriage. What we needed was for me to shut up and pray and wait on the Lord to move. So you see, I am guilty of the same thing. I thank God for His forgiveness, and I have forgiven those who have tried to minister to me without the proper authority from God.

How does someone know when a person is ministering to a troubled individual that it is the will of God for that particular situation? I had an experience that I will never forget. This time, I was doing the ministering to a mother and her teenage child with Tourette's syndrome.

I was leaving the Wednesday night service at church when someone approached me and asked if I would be willing to do a "Missionette overnighter" for a district gathering of girls from around the area because some woman had gotten sick and wouldn't be able to attend. I said yes, and I'm so glad I did. Did I really want to go? Not really. I tend to get tensed up when dealing with a lot of children all at once. But I was told that I'd only be in charge of the girls from my local church, and it helped that my best friend was also attending.

As all the girls and leaders gathered in the gym, where all of the planned activities would take place, my attention was driven to one particular girl. She was about thirteen years old, and she was sitting on the bleachers with all the other girls that were awaiting some event in the gym. She was in the very back row.

What I saw was an exact reflection of me ticking my head and making facial grimaces. I began to wonder if that was why she sat in the very back, where it was the most comfortable for someone who gets stared at constantly. Without any prior knowledge, I was almost convinced that she had the classic symptoms for Tourette's syndrome. I didn't know her name or anything else about her since she was from another church in the district.

The night went on as usual, and I settled in for the evening, getting girls ready for sleeping. I wasn't comfortable at all not sleeping in my own bed but rather on the gym floor with only a sleeping bag for a cushion, and I still had my fear of not sleeping. As God would have it, my best friend ended up sleeping with her girls right next to my group of girls, which gave me emotional comfort. What I didn't know was that God would use me the next morning in a most particular way. It never occurred to me that I would someday wish I could remember every word spoken by the both of us the next day as I finally had the privilege to meet this girl's troubled mother. I cannot say that I remember every detail, but I know enough to be sure that this was a divine setup.

Early the next morning, I found myself in the kitchen, helping to feed the girls a fast and nutritious breakfast of toast and bananas. As I was cutting bananas in half, the subject somehow came up about Tourette's syndrome, and I suddenly found myself face to face with the mother of the girl whom I suspected had it. She indeed did have it, and when this mother found out I had it too and that I'd lived with it most of my life, tears of joy and relief ran down her face.

She had been heartbroken over her circumstances and didn't have any resources to turn to; and there I was to put my arms around her and cry with her, share her burden, and give her some extremely helpful information. Later I also met her daughter and gave her words of comfort. I do know that the Holy Spirit was involved in this meeting in the kitchen. God knew this woman's heartache and worry for her daughter, and He did what He does best, meet us when we need Him desperately. The joy on this woman's face, expressed by her tears of gratitude, was a sign to me that God is never too late; and he always renews our strength, sometimes when we least expect it.

This woman's strength was renewed as I shared my very own personal story with her. She felt hope as she heard the details of my life as a teenager and into adulthood with Tourette's syndrome. By meeting me, she knew that I had survived the experience, and it gave her hope for her daughter. I also spoke to her daughter and encouraged her in her walk with the Lord, and I also let her know that she was valued in spite of her facial grimaces and whatever road she would have to walk down with this disorder called Tourette's syndrome. Unlike some of my past experiences that I've written about in this chapter, I know that God's spirit was upon that meeting in the kitchen that Saturday morning.

The Second Letter to the Corinthians 1:3–4 says, "Blessed be the God and Father of our Lord Jesus Christ, the Father of mercies and God of all comfort, who comforts us in all our tribulation, that we may be able to comfort those who are in any trouble, with the comfort with which we ourselves are comforted by God."

CHAPTER 20

Speaking of Coprolalia:
Do You "Swea?"

One night, when I was eighteen years old, engaged, and stressed to the limit with the symptoms of my then-unknown illness, I caught a bus to take me home after working overtime. As I sat down on the seat, my heart began to beat irregularly and very fast. I became frightened as the bus pulled away, and it got so bad that I stood up and yelled for the bus driver to let me off the bus. I eventually ended up in the hospital ER.

This condition worsened through the years. I was finally diagnosed years later at another ER visit, this one much worse than the first one and all the episodes in between. This time, I was diagnosed with supraventricular tachycardia arrhythmia. After being on the wrong medication (Digoxin) for twenty-three years, I was finally sent to a specialist who put me on the appropriate medicine for the condition.

The doctor was Russian, and he had a rather deep accent. He was very friendly, and I instantly took a liking to him. He noticed on my chart that I had Tourette's syndrome. Immediately after confirming that I indeed did have Tourette's syndrome, he asked me, in his very Russian accent, "Do you swea?" I told him, laughing, that I didn't have that part of the disorder. How quick he was to ask if I swear. He didn't ask what kind of tics I had but instead was just interested as to whether I swore or not. My visit with the Russian doctor stayed friendly, and I told several people about his inquisitiveness into my Tourette's symptoms while imitating his Russian accent as I quoted his question to me.

My interaction with the Russian doctor was pretty comical to me, but while writing this book, I told someone that I had Tourette's syndrome. And their comment to me was something like this, "Oh, don't people with Tourette's swear and say bad things? It's hard to believe you have it." I was kind of taken back and felt misunderstood, but I went on to explain to this uninformed person that only a percentage of people with Tourette's syndrome have coprolalia (involuntary swearing or the utterance of obscene words or socially inappropriate remarks). That ended the discussion.

After that short conversation, I began to wonder just what percentage of people who "know" what Tourette's syndrome is, when asked, really do know. I feel very safe in saying that it's probably one of the most misunderstood disorders. After all, what other neurological disorder causes a person to say socially unacceptable words (coprolalia) or make obscene gestures (copropraxia)?

Although I have not had any of the (coprolalia) or (copropraxia) symptoms, I completely understand the persons with either of these tics because I understand how embarrassing it is to look so unnatural to people as I tic with my facial grimaces. I can't just stop because someone may not understand. The urge is too great most of the time. Bring on the stress of people watching, crowds, noise, and being in a place where one has to stay still (like church); and it's out the window for controlling any tics. At least this is how it is with me most of the time. The world just doesn't understand.

I sometimes wonder why I didn't have coprolalia since I lived amongst people who did swear, such as my own father, and very much. In the projects where I lived as a child, even kids said bad words, but I never even felt the urge to repeat any swear words. For some reason, however, I did have the urge to repeat my brother's name of Pat. I can remember blurting out, "Pa, Pa, Pa, Pa," but never putting the *t* on it. I did this with other people's names and other words also. Now I know why. It was an attempt to hold back from saying the name or word at all, that I was echoing, but I had to say just enough of it to relieve the urge in me.

The urge to want to swear because one is angry and the urge to want to swear when one feels like they will go crazy if they don't are two separate scenarios entirely. I have to admit, I do swear when I get angry even though I profess to be a Christian. I swore before my conversion, and when I get angry, I find that I slip up and swear and have to seek forgiveness from God. But I do not swear as a tic.

In defense of those people who have coprolalia and/or copropraxia, I would like to set the record straight. As controversial as these two conditions of Tourette's syndrome are, I believe that both are as legitimate as any of the other tics of someone with Tourette's. I can understand how some people wouldn't understand these conditions if they've never read any literature or knew anybody with Tourette's syndrome; and that is rather sad for the victim who is seen as a villain to some misunderstanding people in a grocery store, or worse yet, a church service.

I am even more sensitive to this matter now since my encounter with the uninformed person who thought that I swore just because I had Tourette's syndrome. Imagine the heartbreak of the parents of a child who has one or both of these symptoms. Imagine also the child who would give a million bucks not to be the center of attention when making obscene outbursts or gestures where people are watching and judging.

Maybe I shed some light on the subject when I let my Russian doctor know that I don't swear just because I have Tourette's syndrome. Even if he told just one person what he learned that day after talking to me, it would have mattered.

Thinking about all of this would make just about anybody want to swea.

CHAPTER 21

The Cream of the Crop:
Unique and Human

Except for the chapter in which I wrote about my adventurous husband buying a milk truck to take us to Connecticut, I haven't written much about him as it pertains to his coping abilities in living day in and day out with me and with my many complicated issues. When we took our vows after eloping to Vegas, I really didn't know what I was saying when I said, "I will." However, my husband has proven over and over again that when he said, "I will," he meant it.

In the fifty-plus years since then, I have not heard one word or act of regret come from him. Even though we were not then serving the Lord, Lester had qualities that most men in the early seventies did not possess. He was and still is a person of strong character, integrity, and commitment; and I am proud to be his wife.

His love for me is simply selfless, and it has been that way since he proposed to me. To say I am spoiled rotten by him is an understatement, and to say that he is spoiled rotten by me is overkill. When we'd just met, I was going through awful mental difficulty, and as I've explained in this book, this is a problem I've had to deal with throughout my life. In looking back, I think now that I must have been better at hiding my mental status than I thought I was because Lester was either in denial or totally oblivious to my state of mind.

During those years, I began to see him as sort of a father figure, one I could look up to and rely on and one who could eventually fix me to some degree, or at least take the bite out of the misery I was feeling because my earthly father was not there for me. I feel very safe in saying that when it came to my husband, I was mostly gone (as in my own little world); yet his love, commitment, and devotion to me never faltered.

When he was my boyfriend in 1970–1971, my relationship with him was shaping up to be more of one where I could depend on him to solve everyday problems that would come up, like fixing my broken stereo or some relative's broken car because he was already a handyman at the early age of twenty-one. I was already beginning to get spoiled and a little too comfortable because he was all I had to rely on for my sanity, although he couldn't do anything to cure my state of mind in those early days, or even now, fifty years later. After all, my husband didn't give me Tourette's, OCD, depression, and diabetes; and he can't take it away.

It's no wonder that I would come to need him in the way that I did. I had never met anybody like him before, yet I felt I was taking advantage of him because I wasn't sure I loved him. So I felt guilt-ridden. But when I tried to break up with him because I knew it wasn't fair that he should be tied down to a nutcase like me, he refused to let me go.

In my continuing battle with Tourette's syndrome, OCD, and diabetes over the years, Lester has seen me go under the circumstances and into a deep hole many times with depression, withdrawal from life itself. And then at times that I cannot justify for the most part, he has seen me go over the top with my temper and yelling and crying and having my pity parties. He has suffered along with me though my many setbacks from OCD. Yet he has always taken them with a grain of salt, never saying, "Not again" or, "Oh, you'll be all right," but saying instead, "We got through it the last time, and we'll get through this time also." What a husband! It's never me going through something; it's always *we*. His patience level in the times when I need him the most seems to be a ten. If I had to worry about him being mad at me or turning into someone who was very needy like me, I wouldn't have made it. He is a strong, confident, supporting, and a diligent and prayerful Christian husband. I believe that God gave him to me because only He knew what was ahead for me in the years to come.

Oh my, I've just built a perfect husband. I'm sorry. I don't want you to get the idea that my husband is perfect. Far from it! You might be saying, "Lady, do you really know what your husband is?" And the answer is yes. He is human. In fact, he is very human.

He gets mad sometimes; he even yells. Ask the kids about the years when they were growing up at home. Remember the last chapter? He gets impatient at times even when it proves to be futile to do so, like when we're in traffic and someone has cut him off. He'll yell at the bad driver while sitting behind the wheel, and I suddenly get an earful of what this person should have done or not have done to him in traffic.

Oh, and did I mention he is a pack rat? Yes, his shed is filled with stuff that one wouldn't even call junk; but there it is, keeping me from even getting inside if I wanted to (and I don't). He sometimes owns two of the same tools because one is lost in the shed somewhere, and he can't find it, and he has to go buy another one to replace it because it's faster. (Slowly, we are building a small tool business.)

In years past, he has taken up fencing, running, mountain bike riding, racquet ball, and now he plays golf. He even works at play by practicing and reading up on whatever he is pursuing at the time. He is also considered a workaholic by me and most of his friends. He also cannot say no when asked to do something for somebody. One of those times he didn't say no was when my daughter asked him to sew three bridesmaids' gowns from scratch for her wedding. Yes, he sews too and has made his own clothes for the Christian Mountain Man fraternity he used to belong to. He also has carved the most beautiful intricate detailed plaques in his spare time. He is truly a jack-of-all-trades and a master at many.

As a natural handyman, he will always make something rather than buy it. (Remember all the things he made for the milk truck to transform it into a recreational vehicle?) Once, he made a double bed in our living room. Can you, just for a moment, picture your living room filled with electric tools, wood, nails, and sawdust with no room to walk for about two months while a double bed is being built to specification? I can because he did just that for our granddaughters who needed a bed built to fit the space in the room they were sleeping in at the time. This is that part of him that takes things in stride. He never complains about all the work and the time consumption. He just leaves that up to me while he inches toward his many goals and projects. "Need a bed to fit? I can make one." And the stories go on, but my goal here is just to tell you that this is part of the cream that blends in with the human side of my husband.

I wanted you to know more about the man that I eventually did fall in love with, the man who has never been afraid of a challenge, whether it was walking in the worst section of my hometown to come to see me or taking me and our kids to Connecticut in a milk truck or stopping in Vegas to marry me after my very somber display of mental illness. In 2 Timothy 4:7, Paul writes to Timothy, "I have fought the good fight, I have finished the race, I have kept the faith." The race that both my husband and I are running as Christians is not over yet, and I'm not sure of when that race will be over for either one of us. But I am hopeful that we will finish it and will have kept the faith. Part of my husband's race has most definitely been to keep his Faith by being such a committed husband throughout our marriage. The reward comes in 2 Timothy 4: 8 where it says, "Finally, there is laid up for me the crown of righteousness, which the Lord, the righteous judge, will give to me on that day, and not to me only but also to all who have loved His appearing."

EPILOGUE

I'm at the end of my book, and not much has changed. I still have Tourette's syndrome, OCD, depression, and type 1 diabetes; and I have grown older and have more wrinkles and facial hair. Where's the big victory? Did I write this book for nothing? If I did, then I wasted a lot of time and energy.

Let me be the first to tell you that I did not write this book for nothing. I already knew that all of my problems wouldn't disappear just because I'd recorded my life in a book. Yes, writing the book did promote therapy for me at times and made me remember some things that I had forgotten, which made me realize how great God really is. Had I not written this book, I never would have seen this.

This book is not primarily for me but for you the reader. I wrote it because I wanted to share my life and faith in God with you and especially people who have Tourette's syndrome and related disorders. Whether you suffer from this disease or are caring for someone with it, I want you to know that if you are a believer in Christ, hope lies ahead for you no matter what the situation may be.

Help came to me in my deepest and darkest times, but I never realized this until I was able to look back and see how God's righteous right hand was upholding me in many different ways, as evidenced in all the foregoing chapters. I felt calmness and peace when I least expected it but did not yet know that those times were totally and completely a gift from God until I delved into the writing of this book.

I don't have a good singing voice (unless I have the stereo turned up so loud I can't hear myself), but I have learned to sing praises to the Lord when I am at my worst and when every part of my being cries out to shut up. That is when the Lord comes through with the touch of the Holy Spirit, which quickens me and makes me suddenly want to sing. And I'm not just going through the motions, but my heart is in it too. It may not be like that all the time, but it is imperative to just start praising God regardless of what is taking place in your life. I cannot put it any other way than to say that this breaks up that mental scar tissue in your brain and increases your spiritual range of motion. Our goal should be to move freely without the pain of the past, present or future; and I am happy to say that I am finally learning to live one day at a time.

I still have tics and probably always will. I still go through depression, fear, and anxiety; but I have God's Word hidden in my heart now so that I can be comforted by it whenever the need arises. I have found that I feel my best when I am doing things that give me pleasure like being with my grandchildren, writing poetry, journaling in my photo albums, reading my Bible, and exercising. This makes me feel useful and shifts my focus away from myself. This is therapy for me, even if it is hard to take that first step outside of my comfort zone.

Isaiah 40:28–31 says,

> Have you not known? Have you not heard? The everlasting God, the Lord, the Creator of the ends of the earth, neither faints nor is weary. His understanding is unsearchable. He gives power to the weak, and to those who have no might He increases strength. Even the youths shall faint and be weary, and the young men shall utterly fall, but those who wait on the Lord shall renew their strength; they shall mount up with wings like eagles, they shall run and not be weary, they shall walk and not faint.

This verse is powerful. It is true, and it is yours and mine. I know that heaven is the place where all my pain will end for sure. If it happens before that, I will be grateful to God my Father for healing me while still on this planet. For now, I have His grace daily through His comforter, the Holy Spirit, who dwells within me. Psalm 23:1 says, "The Lord is my shepherd; I shall not want."

Isaiah 25:7–8 promises, "And He will destroy on this mountain the surface of the covering cast over all people, and the veil that is spread over all nations. He will swallow up death forever, and the Lord God will wipe away tears from all faces; the rebuke of His people He will take away from all the earth; for the Lord has spoken."

Look back on your life, and you may see as I have that the Lord's hand has always been on you. And remember this promise in Hebrews 13:5: "I will never leave you nor forsake you."

ACKNOWLEDGMENTS

- Tony Shuman, for all those inspiring e-mails, encouragement, and advice, and most of all, for your belief that there was a book in me waiting to be written.
- Jean Shubert, for caring enough to approach me one Sunday in church to inquire about my tumultuous tics and suggesting I see a neurologist for a possible diagnosis of Tourette's syndrome of which I had never heard of. In following your advice, I learned that I did indeed have this disorder.
- Loretta Bailey, for your uncompromising friendship in the last forty-five years, also for your relentless compliments to me about my abilities to do things that I never thought I could. Through thick and thin, you have been there for me. Our friendship is invaluable, and for this, I thank you with all my heart.
- Joanne Backus, for caring enough to count the calories on my plate of those delicious dinners and cookies you made to keep me from blowing it during my complicated pregnancy and for being the wonderful friend you are by lifting me up in prayer numerous times through the years when I had all but crashed. Bless you, dear sister, in the Lord.
- Judy Conroy, loving your neighbor can be a bit of a challenge when you get stuck living next door to someone like me, but you muddled through. And the memories we share (some hilarious) will never fade with time. I can't imagine my life without you in it.

- To my children, Sandra and Mark, for never showing shame of my Tourette's tics and for not being ashamed to bring your friends into our home knowing that they would inevitably ask why I constantly shake my head (and they did), also for putting up with all my idiosyncrasies through the years. You gave me a reason to live in my times of despair. You are both a gift from God, and I love you very much.

- To my husband, Lester, for your unconditional love and acceptance of me and all the baggage I came with from the start. Thank you for never once complaining to me in all the fifty years of our marriage, also for your sizeable patience with me at times when I didn't deserve it and for your necessary help with my book whenever my brain quit. They don't make men like you anymore. I love you very much.

- To the Tourette Syndrome Association Inc. for all I have learned through the years from your organization through group meetings, symposiums, and research information, also for wanting my brain when I am done with it so you just may find something in there to help other patients with Tourette's syndrome after I'm gone.

- Finally, a thank you to God, my Savior, who has been a "lamp unto my feet and a light unto my path" (Psalm 119:106), and I give You all thanks and praise for walking with me through life's journey. You have never failed to rescue me in my darkest hours.

NOTES

1. Tourette's syndrome is a neuropsychiatric, basal ganglia and front cortical circuits, https://pubmed.ncbi.nlm.nih.gov/11587872/#.~:text=
2. Georges Gilles de la Tourette, Executive Summary: Tourette's syndrome, https://www.nndbcom/people/582/000178048?
3. *Random House Webster's College Dictionary Second Edition* (New York: Random House, 1999).

ABOUT THE AUTHOR

Faith Chirillo Stoddard was born and raised in Stamford, Connecticut. At age twelve, she was diagnosed with type 1 diabetes. At age nineteen, she was married and lived in South Carolina for three years. She then moved to Washington state where she now resides with her husband. She is the mother of two children and a grandmother of eight. At age four, she developed what is now known as Tourette's syndrome. She was made fun of in school by her peers because of the many tic movements she exhibited. At age thirteen, she began to have bouts with depression and obsessive compulsive disorder or OCD.

At times, life as she knew it would come to a complete stop as she tried to deal with the depression. Her husband, friends, and family would assist her through these dark times. Her love for children led her to study early childhood education. She thoroughly enjoyed working with special education children and taught first and second grade Sunday School for many years. She was forced to give up teaching because of health issues but enjoys spending time with her grandchildren regularly. She still suffers with Tourette's syndrome, depression, and OCD; but her faith in God, much prayer, and her love for music is what keeps her motivated to continue to be what God has called her to be.

CPSIA information can be obtained
at www.ICGtesting.com
Printed in the USA
BVHW091148130423
662288BV00019B/849